HOSTILE TAKEOVERS

HOSTILE TAKEOVERS

Defence, attack and corporate governance

Tim Jenkinson
Colin Mayer

McGRAW-HILL BOOK COMPANY

London · New York · St Louis · San Francisco · Auckland · Bogotá
Caracas · Lisbon · Madrid · Mexico · Milan · Montreal
New Delhi · Panama · Paris · San Juan · São Paulo · Singapore
Sydney · Tokyo · Toronto

Published by
McGRAW-HILL Book Company Europe
Shoppenhangers Road, Maidenhead, Berkshire SL6 2QL, England
Telephone 0628 23432
Fax 0628 770224

British Library Cataloguing in Publication Data

Jenkinson, Tim
  Hostile Takeovers: Defence, Attack and
  Corporate Governance
  I. Title II. Mayer, C. P.
  333.83

  ISBN 0–07–709029–2

Library of Congress Cataloging-in-Publication Data

Jenkinson, Tim
  Hostile takeovers: defence, attack and
  corporate governance/Tim Jenkinson, Colin Mayer.
    p. cm
  Includes bibliographical references and index.
  ISBN 0–07–709029–2
  1. Consolidation and merger of corporations–Great Britain–Case studies.
  I. Mayer, C. P. (Colin P.) II. Title
  HD2746.55.G3J46   1994
  338.8'3'0941–dc20   94–6127
                                                        CIP

1234 BL 9765

Typeset by TecSet Ltd, Wallington, Surrey
Printed and bound in Great Britain by Biddles Ltd, Guildford, Surrey

CONTENTS

PREFACE

This book grew out of a Special Report that the authors wrote for Oxford Economic Research Associates (OXERA) which looked at the defence strategies that companies used in the event of a hostile takeover bid. The purpose of this book is to give readers an understanding of the way in which 'the market for corporate control' operates in the UK, how this differs across financial systems in other countries, and the approaches that firms have taken to organize takeover defences. By including case studies of all the hostile bids which took place in the UK over a 15-month period it offers an insight into the events surrounding some of the most important takeovers of the past few years.

The book is divided into two parts. In the first part, there is an overview of the takeover market in the UK and an attempt to put the UK market for corporate control into an international context. We suggest that the UK is, in many ways, an outlier compared with other countries, with the management of UK companies being uniquely vulnerable to being ousted against their will. We discuss some of the competing views of the hostile takeover as a method of controlling the management of a company, and suggest some possible ways of balancing the benefits of an active takeover market with the possible costs in terms of long-term corporate performance. The first part also includes a summary of the results that have emerged from the case study analysis.

The results come from an in-depth analysis of 42 case studies of hostile takeovers in the UK over the period January 1989 to March 1990. These are described in the second part, which forms, we believe, one of the largest case study analyses of its type. Understanding the hostile takeover process, and the takeover defences that can be mounted by target firms, requires a detailed knowledge of the background to and events of a takeover. A case study approach is the only way of providing that level of detail. On the other hand, it is not always possible to draw broad conclusions from case studies. By providing evidence on a relatively large number of takeovers we attempt in this book to strike a balance between the benefits of micro-economic evidence and the ultimate desire to draw general policy conclusions. Certainly, we believe that clear trends become apparent in the hostile bids we analyse.

The second part of this book draws heavily on research done by Eric El-Shirbini and Malcolm Hiscock. They worked relentlessly at providing detailed and authoritative case studies. However, the views expressed and any remaining errors are the sole responsibility of the authors.

Tim Jenkinson is a lecturer in Economics at Oxford University and Stock Exchange Fellow at Keble College.

Colin Mayer is Peter Moores Professor of Management Studies at Oxford University and a Fellow of Wadham College.

PART ONE

TAKEOVER DEFENCE STRATEGIES

1

TAKEOVERS IN THE UK

1.1 THE SCALE OF TAKEOVER ACTIVITY

By international standards takeover activity in the UK is high. For example, in 1988 there were 937 takeovers in the UK as against 537 in France and 534 in the then West Germany. In that year the value of takeovers accounted for nearly £17 billion in the UK as against just over £7 billion in France.

While takeover activity is high, it is not consistently so. As Fig. 1.1 illustrates, at the beginning of the 1980s there was a period during which the value of takeover activity was running at around 1 per cent of total stock market value per annum. In comparison, there were peaks in 1972 and 1987–89 when takeovers were running at around 4 per cent of the total UK stock market value. Takeovers therefore come in pronounced waves.

There is little known about these waves, except that they are very closely correlated with stock-market activity. Each of the previous waves coincided with a boom in stock-market prices. It is not quite clear why this is the case but the last takeover wave between 1987 and 1989 gives some clue.

The 1980s' wave was distinctive: while its commencement coincided with a stock-market boom, it continued beyond the stock-market crash of October 1987. This was possible due to the introduction of large-scale debt financing of takeovers, mainly through syndicated bank loans. Without this form of financing the wave of takeovers would have gone away. The previous association of takeover waves with share prices probably therefore reflected the use of equity issues to fund either cash purchases or exchanges of paper.

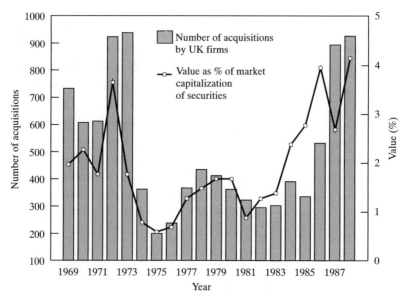

Figure 1.1 Takeovers of UK companies

The 1980s' wave of takeovers died with the failure of a number of highly leveraged deals. This will make banks more cautious about financing large deals in the future. However, alternative financing of takeovers is likely to remain. Increased competition among banks has intensified the search for alternative uses of finance from traditional personal and corporate sector loans. Corporate restructurings are still an attractive proposition, albeit on a more modest scale than before.

However, the factor that is most likely to stimulate takeovers is a growth in stock-market prices. Looking at previous waves suggests that takeovers will not necessarily re-emerge as soon as share prices rise. The 1976 recovery in share prices prompted a surge of new equity issues but not takeovers. It took another 10 years for a takeover wave to reappear. But re-emerge they will. Furthermore, what will distinguish the 1990s from the 1980s is the high level of international takeovers.

Table 1.1 reports the number of international takeovers by, and of, UK companies in 1989 and 1990. It shows that takeovers by UK companies overseas were running at levels that were not too different from total take-over activity in the UK. Furthermore, a significant proportion of takeovers in the UK can be accounted for by overseas takeovers. Thus international takeovers are already an important aspect of the UK takeover market. By all accounts they are set to increase.

The source of the growth is the integration of the European economies and capital markets. As part of the repositioning of firms in the larger European market, major cross-border takeovers have already been

Table 1.1 Cross-border takeovers by, and of, UK firms 1989–90

	1989 Target nationality		1989 Bidder nationality		1990 Target nationality		1990 Bidder nationality	
	Number	Value (£m)	Number	Value (£m)	Number	Value (£m)	Number	Value (£m)
Australia	29	205	3	982	21	81	11	1418
Belgium	34	142	5	2	22	59	5	157
Canada	22	430	8	114	20	757	5	1871
Denmark	5	13	6	122	5	129	9	171
France	77	654	37	3117	66	1683	43	1337
Germany	86	466	16	1181	69	396	26	354
Italy	29	201	3	1	15	140	6	1
Japan	4	72	12	217	0	0	15	1272
Netherlands	89	748	15	263	50	648	22	468
New Zealand	7	124	1	299	5	278	5	1178
Norway	7	4	6	29	2	6	7	32
Spain	38	299	2	48	30	1164	2	0
Sweden	5	5	18	228	7	111	25	2945
Switzerland	7	26	8	613	3	35	13	183
US	262	10 198	51	9171	167	4998	47	1171
Other	63	503	62	1273	53	538	55	1058
Total	764	14 090	253	17 660	535	11 023	296	13 616

observed. The restructuring of corporate Europe is in large part yet to occur. The main innovation that will result is not overseas takeovers of UK firms but large waves of takeovers on continental Europe. The relevance of takeovers will not therefore be limited to the UK during the 1990s.

1.2 THE DEGREE OF HOSTILITY

While the UK has a comparatively high level of takeover activity, that is not its most distinguishing feature. Rather, it is the fact that a significant proportion of all takeover bids are launched *without the agreement of the directors of the target company* that is unusual by international comparison. Indeed, in many cases the management of the target company know nothing about a potential bid until they learn that a (perhaps unknown) investor has accumulated a stake in the company. On other occasions the bidder may pay the target management the courtesy of a phone call before publicly declaring the bid. However, on relatively few occasions do hostile bids result from the breakdown of negotiations aimed at a friendly takeover; more often than not they are a shot from the blue.

There are various ways of defining a hostile bid. In this study we have adopted probably the most common definition: namely that a takeover bid is hostile if the bid is *initially rejected* by the target management. In practice, this definition captures almost all unwelcome bids, since it is virtually unheard of for the management of a target company to accept the offer of a rival bidder immediately without putting up any fight.This definition of a hostile bid would also capture any bid that is initially rejected but *ultimately recommended* by the target management in the course of the bid battle. In the end, target management is often reluctantly forced to accept an offer. However, as the cases reported below record, eventual acceptance says little about the attractiveness of the bid to the target management. Such a reversal in the recommendation of the target management usually occurs only after the initial bid has been increased and when it has become clear that the bid is likely to succeed.

An indication of the frequency of hostile bids can be seen by examining the 10 largest bids (by value) in recent years. As Fig. 1.2 shows, around two-thirds of the largest bids for UK quoted companies were hostile during the 1984–89 takeover wave.

However, hostile takeovers are not restricted to the largest acquisitions. In practice, hostile bids can be launched only for publicly quoted companies (the management of private companies typically hold a large, if not controlling, stake in the equity of their companies). So the most sensible sample to examine in order to determine the incidence of hostile bids is that of companies quoted on the London Stock Exchange. Figure 1.3 documents both the total number of takeovers of quoted companies in each year over the

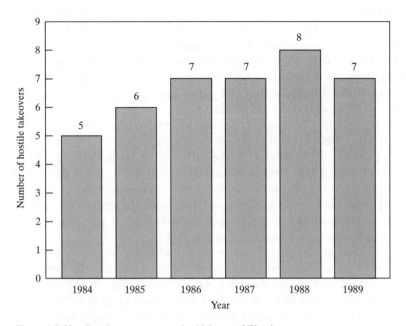

Figure 1.2 Hostile takeovers among the 10 largest UK takeovers

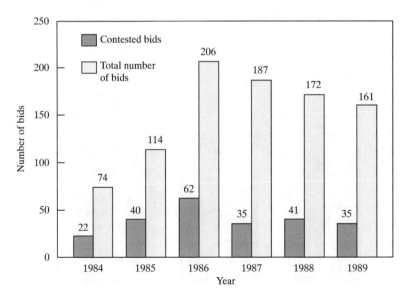

Figure 1.3 Bids for publicly listed targets, 1984–89

period 1984 to 1989 and the number that were hostile according to the definition outlined above. As can be seen, the total number of takeover bids of quoted companies varied quite considerably over the period, rising from just 74 in 1984 to 206 in 1986 (which represented around 10 per cent of all quoted firms in that year). The proportion that were hostile also varied considerably, but over the period as a whole around 26 per cent of the bids for UK quoted companies were hostile.

There is, perhaps, a common perception that hostile takeovers are a product of the 1980s. This is certainly not the case. In Fig. 1.4 we present evidence from the takeover wave in the early 1970s. Again the data refer to takeovers of quoted UK companies, and show that not only was the overall level of takeover activity rather similar to the takeover wave of the late 1980s (at least measured by *number* of bids) but the degree of hostility was also very similar in the two periods, with around 31 per cent of takeovers being hostile at the beginning of the 1970s.

The high level of hostile bids observed in the UK is markedly different from what is found in most other industrialized countries. In Germany, there have been just three reported cases of hostile bids in the whole of the post-Second World War period. In France, until the mid-1980s hostile takeovers were very rare. In Japan hostile bids are also virtually unheard of, with one recent attempt by the famous American corporate raider T. Boone Pickens ending in ignominious failure, after the board of the target company refused to grant Pickens even one board nominee even though he owned over 40 per cent of the equity.

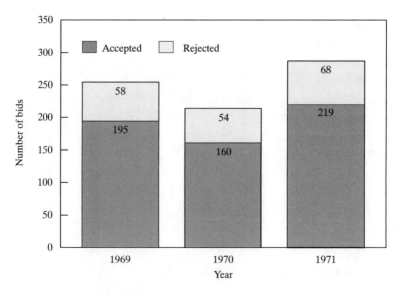

Figure 1.4 Bids for publicly listed targets, 1969–71

A final feature of UK hostile takeovers is noteworthy: contested bids frequently involve more than one bidder. That is, the initial bid quite often attracts one or more additional bidders who submit rival bids to shareholders. Figure 1.5 shows that during the period 1984–89 in just over a quarter of contested bids there was more than one bidder. In comparison, in the 679 uncontested bids over the same period there were just 16 cases of multiple bids.

Multiple bidders can be broken down into three broad categories. First, they can represent the intervention of 'white knights' to protect embattled management. In its purest form, a white knight might make a partial bid for the shares of a company, thus providing protection from other predators but not taking control of the company itself. However, while partial bids are legal in many countries, they are not allowed in the UK. Hence, in practice, any rival bidder must be attempting a complete takeover.

The second type of multiple bidder is the company which enters the battle and gains the recommendation of the target company. In most circumstances, such a rival bidder would have first approached the incumbent management to discuss their entry into the battle and, perhaps, possible reorganizations to be effected in the event of the bid succeeding. However, given that the control of the company will change if the second bidder is successful, such bidders might more accurately be described as *grey knights*: the lesser of two evils.

The third type of multiple bidder is simply another company that enters the battle without the approval—implicit or explicit—of the target company. Such bidders are sometimes referred to as white knights, but in

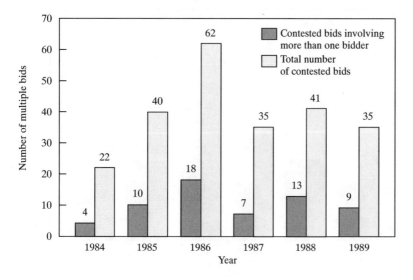

Figure 1.5 Multiple bids for publicly listed targets, 1984–89

practice are simply rivals to the original bidder and are not allies of the target company.

1.3 HOW MANY HOSTILE BIDS SUCCEED?

Consider, to begin with, the outcome of hostile bids involving a single bidder. Figure 1.6 shows the number of contested takeovers involving one bidder that were completed over the period 1984–1989 and the number that failed. As can be seen, in a typical year around one-half of all hostile bids were successful, although in 1984 only 5 of the 18 targets of hostile bids were able to defend themselves successfully. Taking the period 1984–89 as a whole, 55 per cent of the contested bids were completed. At first sight, this would suggest that there is a high success rate for takeover defences. However, as can be seen from Fig. 1.7, if contested takeovers involving more than one bidder are included then the rate of completed takeovers rises to 66 per cent over the sample as a whole.

As can be inferred from Figs 1.6 and 1.7, virtually all bids involving more than one bidder were successful over this period: only 3 of the 61 bids were not completed. Thus, while a high proportion of targets of hostile bids are able to repel the first bidder, in many cases they eventually succumb to another raider. Hostile takeover bids are therefore associated with a high level of ownership changes, albeit not always as a result of the first bid.

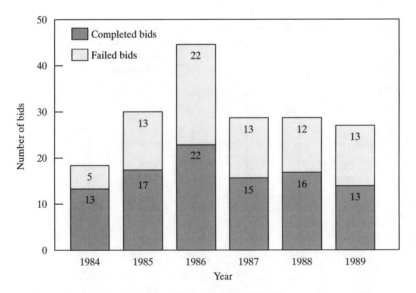

Figure 1.6 Successful and unsuccessful hostile bids, 1984–89

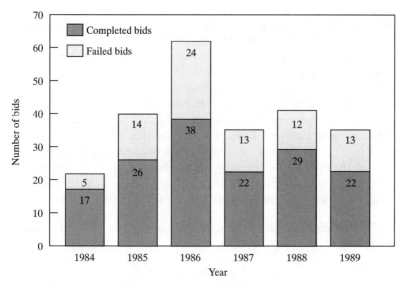

Figure 1.7 Success rate of hostile bids with one or more bidder

1.4 CONTROL CHANGES AND CORPORATE RESTRUCTURING

Not only is there a high level of ownership changes in hostile bids but there is also a high level of control changes. Table 1.2 reports the proportion of executive and non-executive directors that resigned within two years of hostile bids that occurred in 1985 and 1986. It shows that over 70 per cent of target directors of bids that were successfully completed resigned. Where bids failed to be completed it looks as if the rate of resignation is much lower. However, in these cases there appears to be a high rate of resignation in the two years *preceding* a bid.

Table 1.2 Executive replacement in targets of hostile bids, 1985–86

	Proportion of directors of target board who resigned	
	Rejected bids that were nevertheless completed	Rejected bids where the target remained independent
Executive and non-executive directors	78%	33%
Executive directors only	73%	39%

Source: Franks and Mayer (1991).

These executive changes give rise to a high level of control change in target firms. Franks and Mayer (1991) report that in 88 per cent of rejected bids in 1985 and 1986 that were nevertheless completed, target management either did not secure any seats on the main board of the acquiring company or lost their executive chairman in the two years after the bid. Sixty-six per cent of targets failed to retain control on *both* criteria.

One of the consequences of this change in control is a radical restructuring of firms post-takeover. Table 1.3 reports that over 50 per cent of successfully acquired targets of hostile bids disposed of more than 10 per cent of their assets in the two years after acquisition and over 60 per cent underwent significant rationalizations. Even if hostile bids are successfully repelled, rationalizations still occur in nearly 90 per cent of

Table 1.3 Asset disposals and rationalizations in the two years after hostile bids in 1985–86

	Rejected bids that were nevertheless completed	Rejected bids where the target remained independent
Proportion with large asset disposals	53%	32%
Proportion with significant rationalizations	63%	87%

Source: Franks and Mayer (1991).

target firms.

1.5 SUMMARY

This chapter has considered the evidence regarding the extent, and success, of takeovers in the UK over the period 1984–89. To summarize the main findings:

- takeover activity is high in the UK and comes in waves
- takeover waves are closely associated with a buoyant stock market
- a high proportion of takeover activity in the UK is hostile
- hostile bids frequently involve more than one bidder
- in a large proportion of hostile bids changes in ownership eventually occur
- even where targets are able to defend themselves successfully against bids the rate of executive and control change is high.

2

ALTERNATIVE SYSTEMS OF CORPORATE CONTROL

In this chapter we consider a number of related issues. First, we examine the functions of takeovers, in particular hostile takeovers, and review the opposing views regarding the effects of the threat of hostile bids on corporate performance. Second, we place the UK system of corporate control into an international context by examining the ways in which companies are protected from hostile bids in other European Union (EU) countries. We also consider the likely effects of European Commission (EC) harmonization proposals on the market for corporate control in Europe. Third, although the UK and US are often compared in terms of their 'market based' financial systems, we contrast the defensive measures available to management in the US with those permissible in the UK. We conclude that UK companies are uniquely vulnerable to hostile acquisition.

2.1 THE FUNCTION OF TAKEOVERS

Takeovers perform two important functions in an economy. The first is that they allow firms to realize the benefits of economies of large-scale operations. For example, the takeover wave that has been sweeping Europe in recent years has involved the merging of firms, frequently across borders, in preparation for the enlarged European market.

The second function that takeovers perform is to transfer control of unsuccessful firms to successful firms. This function of takeovers is commonly described as the 'market for corporate control'. The term was coined by Henry Manne in 1965 and aptly depicts the way in which many people view this market. According to this description, there is a market for the rights to manage corporate resources in just the way that there is a market in houses, paintings and most other assets. Firms are up for auction to those who wish to take control from existing owners. If bidders attach a higher value to control than the existing owners, then they should be allowed to purchase it. The market in corporate control ensures that firms pass to those who attach the highest value to ownership.

The idea is a very seductive one and it has given rise to a widely held view that the takeover market operates in the national interest. It is a view that has been embraced by governments in several countries, not least recently by the European Union (EU). Vocal supporters of hostile bids are also found within the US. For example, Michael Jensen and Richard Ruback wrote in 1983:

> The market for corporate control is creating large benefits for shareholders and for the economy as a whole by loosening control over vast amounts of resources and enabling them to move more quickly to their highest-valued use. This is a healthy market in operation... and it is playing an important role in helping the American economy adjust to major changes in competition and regulation of the past decade.

Such is the force of these arguments that attempts by managers to impede the process are frequently viewed as being self-serving and operating against the interests of the ultimate owners of the firm, namely the shareholders. There is no question that this can indeed be the case. However, there are two reasons why this is not necessarily the case. The first is that takeover defences may be required to allow companies to implement long-term investment strategies and the second is that takeovers may act against the interests of other stakeholders in the firm. We consider these issues in the next section.

2.2 THE COSTS OF HOSTILE BIDS

One of the observations that was made in Chapter 1, and will be considered in detail in Part 2, was that takeovers frequently give rise to substantial policy changes in the form of changes in control, asset disposals and restructurings. In some cases these policy changes are indisputably warranted by the poor past performance of firms. But elsewhere there is the possibility that an active market for corporate control may result in too many changes of policy.

The analogy that can be made here is with an army in battle that determines the day's strategy by taking a vote among its soldiers. In one respect this can only be to the benefit of those who are most affected by decisions taken. In another it is clearly likely to give rise to too little consistency in strategy from day to day. The mood of the troops may be too vulnerable to extraneous considerations; the outcomes of votes may be determined by shifting coalitions between particular groups; and most troops may be quite ignorant about strategy. Far better to leave strategy up to a small group of experts.

But there is a still more serious risk of having too liberal a system of corporate control: those who invest the most in their companies may be the most vulnerable to hostile takeovers. Unless they specify otherwise, the owners of a British company have full rights to treat their property as they wish, providing of course that their actions fall within the letter of the law. This includes the right to dispose of assets and close plants.

In normal circumstances, employees and managers do not have any control rights in the operation of their firm, save that contracts that are agreed with existing owners in general become the responsibility of new owners. There is therefore nothing that ensures that what is in the interests of the *shareholders* is in the interests of other *stakeholders*—employees, pensioners, suppliers, etc.

Not only may this be unfair, it may undermine the long-term operation of firms. If employees cannot be sure that when control changes occur they will be adequately rewarded for past investments that they have made, in, for example, training then they may be unwilling to undertake it in the first place. Likewise, if managers do not expect to reap the benefits of long-term high-risk strategies because raiders compete the gains away, then they will choose safer, short-term strategies. Thus it may be necessary for employees and managers to be afforded a measure of protection to induce them to make long-term investments in a firm.

A popular way of describing these problems is that a hostile takeover bid may lead to a breach of an *implicit contract*. As their name suggests, implicit contracts are understandings based on *trust* and, unlike explicit contracts, have no standing in law and cannot be enforced through courts. Implicit contracts can take various forms, involving different stakeholders in the company. Two examples should make the issues clear.

First, consider the decision of a skilled employee to work for a particular company. This decision is, in many ways, an investment decision: he decides to invest his human capital in the specific activities of the company. He will expect the investment to pay off in time: he will want to be rewarded financially, to be promoted and to have continuous employment unless he fails to perform his prescribed duties (he may also have other expectations, such as his pension rights increasing with inflation). *Ex ante*, such contracts can be mutually beneficial to the employee and shareholder alike. However, *ex post*, it can be value maximizing for shareholders to break the implicit contracts, for example by raiding the pension fund or laying off skilled workers. Hostile bids, it could be argued, present an opportunity for one set of shareholders (who, collectively, may have honoured the implicit contracts) to be replaced by a single shareholder who may, in the short-term at least, see the opportunity to increase profits by breaking the implicit contracts.

Once employees and other stakeholders cease to trust shareholders, they will not enter into implicit contracts, and an environment of suspicion and distrust will tend to emerge. Stakeholders will insist upon detailed explicit contracts, and, since negotiating explicit contracts can be costly, stakeholders may demand premiums on such contracts. Life becomes more litigious. In essence, once there is a fear that corporations cannot be trusted, there will be a decline in corporate loyalty, which will affect even those corporations which have never violated implicit agreements. Thus, the threat of hostile takeovers acts as an unfavourable externality on an economy, and results in welfare losses to society.

The second example concerns the relationship between companies, such as a final producer and its suppliers. It is common for a supplier—for example a components supplier—to have to invest in specific capital equipment (such as tooling) in order to produce a particular intermediate good for a final producer. Such investments are often sunk, or at least have a much reduced value in alternative uses. As a result, once the investment has been made the supplier becomes extremely vulnerable to opportunistic behaviour by the final producer. The latter may renege (or threaten to renege) on an agreement, or attempt to push down the price that it pays for the components. Of course, such possibilities would in general provide incentives to formalize any business relationship in an explicit contract. However, enforcing contracts through courts is, in general, costly, slow and cumbersome.

A good example of the problems observed in practice in maintaining a business relationship based upon a formal contract was the protracted dispute between Eurotunnel and Trans-Manche Link. The latter had a contract to build the tunnel between France and the UK, which Eurotunnel was then responsible for operating. However, as with most contracts, it was not possible *ex ante* to build all possible contingencies into the contract. Specifications changed, unexpected conditions were encountered during the tunnelling, etc. As a result, both parties spent considerable periods of time in costly disputes which were characterized by their acrimonious and hostile nature.

These transactions costs may push companies towards establishing business relationships upon implicit agreements, which are usually long-term and based upon mutual trust. Kester (1992) characterizes the issue as follows: 'The central problem of governance is to devise specialised systems of incentives, safeguards, and dispute resolution processes that will promote the continuity of business relationships that are efficient in the absence of self-interested opportunism.' Governance of this type—which has been termed *contractual governance*—is clearly quite different from the more general issues of corporate governance, which are associated, essentially, with the potential principal–agent problems resulting from the separation of ownership and control.

Systems of contractual governance differ significantly across countries. At one extreme might lie the US, where companies rely extensively on explicit contracts and, in the event of disputes, the courts. At the other extreme, German and Japanese companies typically rely upon implicit contracts, reinforced by long-term relationships which build up trust between the parties involved. Disputes are typically resolved without recourse to courts, with each party being aware of the value of the continuing relationship, which would be jeopardized by opportunistic or unreasonable behaviour by any one party.

Hostile takeover bids can be examples of such opportunistic behaviour. Long-term business relationships between companies are built upon trust; in particular trust between the management teams. In most cases, a hostile bidder (who introduces a new management team) will have had no previous business relationship with any of the upstream or downstream companies, and so will not be able to reap the potential benefits of implicit contracting. Indeed, in some cases the hostile bidder may choose to take advantage of the vulnerable position of, say, suppliers and force down the prices paid for the components. This may raise short-term profits, but destroy the system of contractual governance, and push all parties towards more explicit contracting.

Worse still, if hostile bids are widespread in an economy, it may be impossible for *any* companies to enter into the kind of long-term relationship outlined above, built on implicit contracts, however much the management teams of each company would, individually, like to build up such relationships. The reason is clear: if the incumbent management team is vulnerable to a hostile bid, it cannot commit any potential hostile bidder to honouring the implicit contracts and not breaking the trust between the two parties. As a result, contracts will have to be more explicit, fewer companies will rely upon verbal assurances and trust, and the benefits of long-term relationships between companies will be less apparent. Hostile takeovers, according to this view, again impose an externality on the corporate sector as a whole.

In short, while the threat of a hostile bid may provide an important incentive for the incumbent management of firms to be efficient, and to pursue policies that are in their shareholders' interests, the existence of such hostile bids may have more widespread implications for the way in which business relationships are conducted in an economy. When the threat of a hostile takeover exists it may be impossible to establish and maintain long-term relationships built upon trust and implicit contracts, which may result in less efficiency. This applies equally well for the relationships between companies and their employees (including the management team) and for the relationships between different companies. Any analysis of the relative merits of hostile bids compared to other systems of corporate governance should compare the benefits and the costs for different types of firms.

2.3 HOSTILE TAKEOVERS IN THE EUROPEAN UNION (EU)

The UK system of corporate control—in particular the role of the hostile takeover—is often compared unfavourably with those in existence in other EU countries and elsewhere. UK quoted companies frequently cite the takeover threat as a serious impediment to investing, particularly in R&D related projects. Instead, it is argued, companies are expected to pay out a large proportion of their earnings as dividend payments in order to avert the threat of a hostile bid. This broad set of complaints has come to be known as the charge of *short-termism* and has become a popular catch-all indictment of the entire UK financial system, albeit one that remains to be proved.

These criticisms are heard not only from within the UK. There is a deep philosophical divide between the UK and the rest of the EU regarding who should ultimately control a company. The UK system is relatively simple to characterize: accountability of management to the shareholder is paramount. The shareholders ultimately own the assets of the company, and it is they who should have the right to decide which management team should have the right to use the assets on their behalf. The threat of a hostile takeover is an essential part of the process of ensuring that managers are efficient and maximize shareholder value.

In contrast, the purpose of 'the company' in most other EU countries is not so straightforward. Shareholders are clearly one interest group, but many others exist: workers, the existing management, suppliers, providers of finance other than shareholders (such as banks), and other related companies. Such groups are often referred to as *stakeholders* in a company—those who are involved in the day-to-day operations and who in most EU countries have a right to play a part in the process of controlling the company.

The different philosophies have deep historical roots, and this is certainly not the place to trace such ancestry. However, the diverse systems of corporate control in the EU sit somewhat uncomfortably within the concept—if not the reality—of the single European market. If product markets should be open to all companies within the EU, why should companies themselves not be bought and sold freely, including the right to offer to buy a company against the wishes of the existing management? At the very least, perhaps, there should be some equality of treatment between EU countries, so that a

UK company should have the same ability to be the predator as well as the prey.

The result has been the long-standing attempt by the European Commission to harmonize various aspects of the law regarding takeovers. The road to harmonization is seldom particularly smooth, but in few areas has the EU encountered as many obstacles as in the case of takeovers. This is not altogether surprising, however, once one acknowledges the philosophical divide over the role of the company.

2.3.1 How are companies protected?

A distinction is often drawn between *structural* and *technical* barriers to takeover. Structural barriers reflect the particular way companies grow, are owned, and are financed in different countries. Such barriers, therefore, result from the underlying structure of the economy, including such diverse factors as the distribution of wealth, the role of institutions (in particular financial institutions) and the political system.

In contrast, technical barriers are typically erected by companies themselves—through, for example, regulations limiting voting rights—or through laws which give considerable power to parties other than shareholders, such as existing managers, workers or second-tier boards of directors. The purpose of technical barriers is to limit the ability of a potential predator to mount a successful hostile bid for a company, or to increase the cost of making such a bid.

While the attempt at harmonizing EU takeover legislation has concentrated on technical barriers to takeover, it is arguable that structural barriers normally present the greatest barrier to a takeover, and it is to these that we turn first.

2.3.2 Structural barriers

In looking at the financing of companies in different EU countries, and the development of their financial systems, one is struck more by the differences than by the similarities. Perhaps the most important difference between countries is simply the size of the quoted sector. Since it is only quoted companies that can, potentially at least, be subjected to a hostile takeover bid, the size of the quoted sector will be an important indicator of the structural barriers existing in different countries.

As Fig. 2.1 shows, with the exception of Luxembourg, the size of the UK quoted sector is much higher as a proportion of GDP than any other EU country. Whereas in the UK the market capitalization of quoted firms represented (in 1990) over three-quarters of annual GDP, in the four other large economies—Germany, France, Italy and Spain—the quoted sector accounted for less than one-quarter of annual income. This tendency

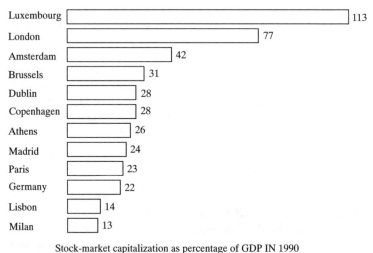

Stock-market capitalization as percentage of GDP IN 1990

Figure 2.1 Size of the quoted sector in EU countries

for companies to remain private constitutes by far the greatest structural barrier to a hostile bid.

However, in most EU countries, even within the quoted sector, a company with a majority of its shares in public hands is a rarity. Shareholding tends to be much more concentrated. Families frequently retain control of a company even when it becomes quoted. For example, Coopers & Lybrand (1989) found family holdings to be important in many EU member states, in particular Italy and Spain. In the case of Italy, it was estimated that of the 200 quoted companies only 7 had more than half of their equity in public hands, and so could in principle be the subject of a hostile bid.

State ownership often presents an additional source of structural barriers. This is particularly important in the case of France, where more than half the quoted firms are family controlled and the state holds controlling stakes in many of the remainder.

However, a variety of other structural barriers to takeover are found in EU countries. Financial institutions play very different roles in different countries. Debt finance is relied upon more extensively in most EU countries than in the UK. This is particularly true of relatively small, growing companies. Whereas in the UK companies tend to raise equity finance relatively early, by going public, in most other EU countries there is a tendency to rely upon bank finance for longer, and, as Fig. 2.1 demonstrates, to remain unquoted. The nature of financial markets and institutions may, therefore, be as much a contributor to structural barriers as anything else.

However, the importance of financial institutions is not limited to their role in providing finance; they often play a direct role in controlling quoted companies as well. The most widely cited example is that of the German bank. Not only do German banks hold significant amounts of equity in their own right, but they are frequently given the power to vote on behalf of individual shareholders who surrender their proxies. The custom of depositing shares at banks results from the issuing of shares in bearer form.

The potentially important role played by German banks can be illustrated by one of the few recorded cases of a hostile bid for a German firm. As Franks and Mayer (1990) report, during the 1988 bid for Feldmüle Nobel AG it was estimated that Deutsche Bank held proxy voting rights for around 55 per cent of Feldmüle's equity. As a result the bid (which was for only 51 per cent of the shares) failed. Deutsche Bank then supported a management proposal to restrict the voting rights of any individual investor to 5 per cent. It is interesting, however, that such restrictions do not typically apply to the proxy votes controlled by banks, which again augments the importance of their role in controlling companies.

All these, and other, forms of structural barrier are unlikely to be affected by any of the proposals to harmonize takeover legislation. This is not only inevitable—since it is not clear what legislation could be effective—but also appropriate, for the following reasons. First, if one particular control structure produces a less efficient management than some other then there will be an incentive for the owners of the company to change the system of control by, for example, going public or reducing the concentration of ownership. Second, in concentrating on the market for corporate control it is important not to lose sight of the product market. An inefficiently managed company is unlikely to survive in a competitive market, and the pressures of product market competition may be as effective at disciplining managers as any discipline exerted through financial markets.

2.3.3 Technical barriers

A voluminous literature exists on the extent of technical barriers to takeover in the EU (see for example Coopers & Lybrand (1989) or Booz Allen (1989)). Technical barriers are concerned explicitly with the allocation of the power to control a company, and are typically enshrined in company statute or result from national regulations defining, for example, the rights of various stakeholders.

Numerous technical barriers to takeover have been found in many EU countries other than the UK. The most important of these are the following.

1. *Voting restrictions*—in particular, limitations on the number of votes that can be cast by any individual shareholder.
2. *Dual class shares*—by issuing shares with low (or no) voting rights, the original owners of the company can often effectively retain control.

3. *Transfers of shares*—these can be restricted (for example, transfers to foreigners may be limited) or may require the approval of the board.
4. *Two-tier boards*—the executive board of a company is often appointed by a supervisory board. The replacement of the executives can only be made by the supervisory board, on which employees often have a right to representation (for example employees are entitled to 50 per cent representation on the supervisory boards of large German companies). Such two-tier board structures can make it extremely difficult to replace the existing management.
5. *Super-majority clauses*—these can be applied to certain decisions, such as a takeover bid or the removal of the existing management. Under such arrangements certain proposals may require, say, 80 per cent of the votes before they are accepted.

A final consideration that has been important both elsewhere in the EU and in Japan is the widespread use of cross-shareholding agreements. While such arrangements—whereby companies agree to build up equity stakes in each other—are normally justified on grounds other than as a takeover barrier (such as the development of joint ventures), their effect is often to consolidate control in the hands of a friendly shareholder. Such control is seldom complete—a 10 per cent cross-shareholding is quite typical—but such arrangements none the less introduce an additional barrier to a hostile bid.

An example of such arrangements involving a UK company is that between *Guinness* and *LVMH* of France. Initially the two companies bought 12 per cent of each other's shares; this was later increased to 24 per cent. Such arrangements are somewhat different to most of the other technical barriers mentioned above. First, they would normally require shareholder approval. Second, they can be undone if the purported benefits are not forthcoming, or if the incumbent management abuses the added protection afforded by the cross-shareholding. Third, they are seldom an absolute barrier to a hostile bid, particularly as many countries put limits on the size of minority stakes that can be accumulated without making a full bid for the company.

We would argue that the most important consideration in this respect is the ability of shareholders to *approve* any takeover barrier that is put in place. A key objection to many of the technical barriers mentioned above is that they are designed simply to remove power from some shareholders and entrench the power of others. However, if there is validity in the claim that the existence of a threat of hostile acquisition reduces the ability of the existing management to maximize the long-term value of the firm, then there is no reason why shareholders should not approve the erection of some limited defence. In this case, technical barriers that are approved, and periodically reviewed, by shareholders—such as cross-shareholdings—

should simply be viewed as a voluntary contractual arrangement, and should not be the subject of legislation.

2.3.4 European Commission (EC) harmonization proposals

The long-standing attempt of the European Commission (EC) to harmonize takeover law is currently summarized in two documents: the *Thirteenth Directive on Company Law, concerning Takeover and Other General Bids*, and the *Proposal for a Regulation on the Statute for a European Company*.

Broadly speaking, the *Thirteenth Directive* is concerned with takeover defences. It focuses on the actions available to the management of a target company in the event of a hostile bid, and the rules by which a bid battle should be fought. A critical stumbling block has been the proposal that the Directive would be implemented by statute, rather than through a non-statutory self-regulatory body such as the Takeover Panel. The main concerns over any statutory system are that it would lack the necessary flexibility and would increase the likelihood of the whole takeover process being submerged in litigation. Since any ruling could be challenged in both national and European courts, tactical litigation as a takeover defence—as is commonplace in the US—would be the likely outcome in many cases. Although decisions of the Takeover Panel are subject to judicial review, to date only three decisions have been reviewed, and in each case the Panel's decision has been upheld.

In contrast to the *Thirteenth Directive*, the *Statute for a European Company* considers the defences which companies can erect *before* a bid takes place. As noted above, extensive technical barriers to takeover exist in many EU countries. However, the *Statute for a European Company* does not go far in its attempts to harmonize the use of pre-bid defences. For example, while the issue of dual classes of equity would be disallowed, a company would still be free to impose limits on the number of votes that could be cast by any individual shareholder.

What impact, then, would the proposed EC legislation have on UK companies? It is tempting to view the harmonization proposals as 'all sound and fury signifying nothing'! Given the importance of structural barriers to takeover—which would be completely unaffected by the EC proposals—the downside risks facing the UK seem to dominate any possible upside gains. Relatively few EU companies would become much more open to hostile acquisition even if the current proposals were implemented in full. Even for the minority of companies that currently rely upon technical barriers, significant pre-bid defences will remain available. However, the UK risks losing a proven system of takeover regulation that is generally perceived as both fair and efficient.

It is interesting in this respect to compare the range of technical defences that are widely used by US companies, and it is to this that we now turn.

2.4 US-STYLE DEFENSIVE MEASURES

The UK and US financial systems are often held up as being the prime examples of 'market based' systems. In some respects this is obviously the case: there are a large number of quoted companies, and banks play a relatively minor role in both financing and controlling companies. In both countries there is a general absence of controlling stakes owned by families, the state, or other companies or financial institutions. As a result, there are a large number of hostile bids, suggesting a relatively free market for corporate control.

However, there are very great differences in the ability of companies to protect themselves from a hostile bid between the two countries. In the case of the UK it is clear that companies have relatively few defences available in the event of a hostile bid. Target companies are typically limited to financial announcements (such as updated dividend or profit forecasts); disposals or revaluations of assets; appeals to the various regulators, or finding a white knight. However, with the exception of the white knight, these defences are rather weak, especially in the case of a cash bid. There are relatively few examples in recent years of hostile cash bids failing to succeed, except when a white knight was prepared to enter the auction.

In contrast, the defences available to US companies are quite extensive. These include the following:

1. *Charter amendments*, such as super-majority amendments, staggered board provisions (whereby a new majority shareholder would be unable to gain control of the board for a number of years), and preferred stock authority (whereby the management is authorized to issue new shares with disparate voting rights to 'friendly' parties).
2. *Poison pills*, the most important of which are *flip-overs*—which are essentially options to purchase, at a significant discount, shares in the combined firm in the event of a successful hostile bid—and *ownership flip-ins*—which entitle shareholders of a target company to purchase additional shares in the company at a discount once a hostile bidder has accumulated more than a certain proportion of the equity (often 30 per cent).
3. *Greenmail*, or targeted share repurchases, whereby a target firm buys back the shares of a hostile bidder, typically at a premium. The important aspect of greenmail—which connotes blackmail—is that the management only offer to buy back the shares of the bidder, and the premium price is, effectively, paid by all other shareholders. Greenmail is often accompanied by a standstill agreement, whereby the bidder agrees not to gain control of the company for a specified period.

4. *Litigation*, which is an available defence in many countries, although is particularly important in the US and particularly weak in the UK, given the self-regulatory role played by the Takeover Panel.

Such defensive measures are widely used in the US. For example, by January 1988 around 560 firms had employed poison pill defences, the vast majority of which were either flip-overs or ownership flip-ins. Some of the defensive measures can clearly act against shareholder interests. This is often supported by the empirical evidence. For example, a study of targeted share repurchases and standstill agreements found that the share prices of firms employing such defensive tactics fell by around 4 per cent on their announcement (Dann and DeAngelo, 1983).

However, many of these technical barriers required shareholder approval before they could be adopted. For example, proposed charter amendments require shareholder approval, which, in the majority of cases, is forthcoming. Why would shareholders agree to such restrictions on takeovers unless they were in the interests of the company? The empirical evidence on the effect of anti-takeover charter amendments on share prices is not conclusive: early studies suggested that, if anything, the value of the company tended to *rise* on the adoption of charter amendments (see for example Linn and McConnell, 1983). However, more recent studies have produced conflicting results, with small (around 1 per cent) reductions in the share price being observed on average (see for example Jarrell and Poulsen, 1987). At present, therefore, it is hard to draw conclusions on the effect of such takeover protection on existing shareholders.

The interesting unresolved issue is whether, for certain types of firm, some additional protection would be in the long-term interests of both the existing management and the shareholders. Obviously, the prospect of shareholders being offered a bid premium would be reduced, but the ability of management to maximize the long-term value of the firm may be enhanced by some additional security of tenure. It is worth noting in passing that, to date at least, the shareholders in *Guinness* have enjoyed a considerable increase in the value of their holdings since the adoption of the cross-shareholding agreement with *LVMH*.

2.5 SUMMARY

The debate over takeovers, and corporate governance more generally, is likely to continue on the EU and domestic UK fronts. In this chapter we have reviewed some of the major issues, and considered the various policy proposals. The main conclusions we would draw are as follows.

First, it is well known that UK companies are uniquely vulnerable within the EU to hostile takeover. However, it would be wrong to attribute the unevenness of this particular playing field solely to the existence of technical barriers to takeover. Structural barriers—which have complex historical and institutional roots—are typically far more important in explaining the protected position of many EU companies. Such barriers would, quite rightly, be completely untouched by attempts at EC harmonization.

Second, while the attempts at EC harmonization of takeovers have currently stalled, it is not clear that the proposed measures would go far in opening up EU companies to hostile acquisition. The philosophical divide regarding the role of 'the company' is unlikely to be bridged by attempts at harmonization. In addition, one real fear for the UK is that the system of takeover regulation proposed by the EC could significantly reduce the efficiency of the takeover process compared to current practices in the UK.

Third, it is perhaps commonplace to think of the UK and the US as the leading examples of market based financial systems, including a relatively free market in corporate control. However, we have argued that US companies have many more takeover defences available to them than their UK counterparts. These technical defences are used very widely, and suggest that companies are more open to hostile acquisition in the UK than in *any* other major economy.

Finally, a somewhat contentious question was raised: is there a case for certain companies—perhaps those with large R&D expenditures—to be able to erect some limited technical barriers to takeover? This is especially relevant in countries such as the UK where very few structural barriers to takeover exist. This would clearly move the UK system towards current practice in the US, where the available evidence suggests that certain types of takeover defence are not necessarily against shareholders' interests. The recent participation by a few UK companies in cross-shareholding agreements with other EU companies suggests that such technical barriers are starting to emerge. Provided such defences are approved by shareholders and are reviewed at regular intervals they may be in the interests of all parties concerned.

We suggest that there can be no presumption that unfettered markets for corporate control are always appropriate. There are circumstances in which markets for corporate control should quite appropriately be restrained to provide adequate incentives to invest. The risk is that management will thereby become complacent and corporate performance will deteriorate. There is therefore a trade-off between the disciplinary effect of takeovers and their disruptive impact on investment and long-term growth. In some industries, the former will probably outweigh the latter and impediments to takeovers will be harmful. Elsewhere, in particular where the level of investment required of management and workers is high, impediments to takeovers may well serve a valuable function.

3

DEFENCE STRATEGIES

The second part of this book records the results, in detail, of a study of the 42 hostile bids that occurred over the period January 1989 to March 1990 (excluding takeovers of investment trusts which are not studied in this report). This period was chosen as being the most recent one of active takeover activity in the UK.

The takeovers are listed in chronological order in Table 3.1, in which the bidder, the target, the date of the bid and the size of the bid are also recorded. Targets of contested takeovers tend to be slightly larger than those of friendly takeovers and, in particular, targets of failed contested takeovers are larger than those of friendly takeovers (Franks and Mayer, 1991).

The largest bid by far in our sample was that by *Hoylake* for *BAT* which was valued at £13.5 billion. The next largest was the *Hanson* bid for *Consolidated Gold Fields*, for £3.5 billion. Other prominent bid battles over the period included the successful bid for *Ward White* by *Boots*, the unsuccessful bid for *Dixons* by *Kingfisher*, and the interesting bid for *Gateway* which became an intense battle between rival bidders *Isosceles* and *Newgateway*.

The approach of the analysis has been to examine the bids on an individual case-by-case basis. For each case, background information on the financial performance of the target was collected. Information on earnings per share, dividends per share and share prices was collected. The activities of the bidder and the target were determined from company accounts and listings of the industrial composition of firms.

Table 3.1 Takeovers studied (in chronological order)

Target	Bidder	Announcement	Bid value (£m)
Bassett Foods	Procordia A.B. (Sweden)	12 Jan. 1989	53.0
Ricardo Group	First Technology	20 Jan. 1989	22.7
Marina Development Group	Local London Group	7 Feb. 1989	77.7
Chamberlain Phipps	Bowater Industries	21 Feb. 1989	86.6
Local London Group	Priest Marians Holdings	21 Feb. 1989	111.0
Boase Massimi Pollitt	Boulet Dru Dupuy Petit	29 Mar. 1989	118.0
Lambert Howarth Group	Peter Black Holdings	10 Apr. 1989	9.3
Piccadilly Radio	Miss World Group	13 Apr. 1989	39.3
Gateway Corporation	Isosceles	18 Apr. 1989	2050.0
Habit Precision Engineering	Epicure Holdings	21 Apr. 1989	10.7
Ketson	Moneytab	22 May 1989	2.8
Coalite Group	Anglo United	24 May 1989	478.0
Business Mortgages Trust	National Home Loans	5 June 1989	13.3
Molins	IEP Securities	13 June 1989	68.8
Consolidated Gold Fields	Hanson Trust	22 June 1989	3500.0
Red Funnel	Sally Holdings UK	23 June 1989	24.0
Ward White Group	Boots	3 July 1989	900.0
BAT Industries	Hoylake	11 July 1989	13500.0
Tilbury Group	Lilley	13 July 1989	137.0
A Goldberg & Sons	Blacks Leisure Group	31 July 1989	32.0
De La Rue	Norton Opax	21 Aug. 1989	586.0
Norton Opax	Bowater Industries	4 Sept. 1989	384.6
United Scientific Holdings	Meggitt	11 Sept. 1989	93.4
Armstrong Equipment	Caparo Group	14 Sept. 1989	98.7
Meat Trade Suppliers	Twigrealm	21 Sept. 1989	9.2
DRG	Pembridge Investments	26 Sept. 1989	697.0
Pearl Assurance Group	Australian Mutual Provident	2 Oct. 1989	1240.0
Higgs & Hill	Y J Lovell	20 Nov. 1989	155.0
Hestair	Adia Group (Switzerland)	20 Nov. 1989	167.0
Metal Closures Group	Wassall	30 Nov. 1989	45.9
Dixons	Kingfisher	6 Dec. 1989	568.0
Colonnade Development Capital	Stratagem Group	22 Dec. 1989	8.2
Hartwell	Oakhill	4 Jan. 1990	172.4
Norfolk Capital Group	Queens Moat Houses	25 Jan. 1990	184.0
Chemoxy International	MTM	2 Feb. 1990	11.8
Laing Properties	Pall Mall Properties	5 Feb. 1990	492.0
Sketchley	Godfrey Davis	12 Feb. 1990	138.0
Walter Runciman	Forvaltnings Avena (Sweden)	23 Feb. 1990	63.5
Camford Engineering	Markheath Securities	1 Mar. 1990	63.8
Sketchley	Compass Group	8 Mar. 1990	106.0
Molins	Leucadia National Corporation (US)	28 Mar. 1990	83.0
Crystalate Holdings	TT Group	30 Mar. 1990	32.5

Each case was examined and recorded in a systematic fashion. Firstly, the events leading up to the bid were recorded. This included the announcement of the bid and the offer made by the bidder. Then the response of the target in making a defence against the bid was examined. Finally, the outcome of the bid has been noted.

The cases are reported in Part 2. Each case is set out with summary information at the beginning on the target, the bidder, their activities, the date of the announcement of the bid, the value of the bid, the defences employed (classified according to five categories that are described in the next section), the outcome of the bid and then a summary of the bid itself. The detailed description of each case is set out as the background, the defence, the outcome, the financial performance of the target and the share-price performance relative to the FT index.

3.1 ALTERNATIVE DEFENCE TACTICS

The responses of companies to hostile bids are many and varied. However, although the specific action taken by target firms varies considerably, there is a remarkable similarity in the types of responses observed. As a result, it is possible to classify virtually all the defence tactics employed into five broad categories, with relatively few special cases failing to sit comfortably within these summary categories. The five main categories we employ—and their associated sub-categories—are presented in Table 3.2. We shall discuss

Table 3.2 Classification of UK defence tactics

Main categories	Sub-categories
Financial responses	Profits announcements Dividend announcements Asset revaluations
Corporate restructurings	Asset disposals Changes in management Management buy-outs
White knights	
Poison pills	
Legal and/or political	Appeals to: Office of Fair Trading Courts Takeover Panel Stock Exchange Overseas authorities Politicians

each of these in turn, drawing examples from the case studies presented in Part 2.

3.1.1 Financial responses

One of the most common responses of firms to threatened takeovers is to make an announcement concerning current and prospective financial performance. This can relate to profits, dividends or the value of assets.

Profits announcements are most prominent of these. *Ward White* announced an increase in its interim pre-tax profits of 19 per cent over the previous year during the course of a bid from *Boots* in July 1989. Under threat from *Sally Holdings* in June 1989, *Red Funnel* announced a rise of 14 per cent in interim pre-tax profits and forecast an increase of 13 per cent for the year as a whole.

While most announcements are of higher than anticipated profits, in a few cases profits have been revised downwards. An example of this occurred during *Godfrey Davis'* bid for *Sketchley* in February 1990. *Sketchley* announced pre-tax profits of £6 million as against a forecast of £14.8 million for the year to March 1990. This was down from £17.3 million in the previous year.

Sketchley revised profits downwards further the following month when it was subject to a second bid from *Compass*. On this occasion, it revealed costs for defence against the *Godfrey Davis* bid of £1.2 million and further costs associated with the resignation of the chairman on announcement of the *Compass* bid.

Another example of a company making an announcement of reduced future profitability was *United Scientific Holdings'* response to a bid by *Meggitt* in September 1989. *USH* doubled provisions for losses and potential write-offs on fixed price contracts to £17 million. Even though *Meggitt* received acceptances from a majority of shareholders, it decided not to declare the offer unconditional.

Dividend announcements: Announcements of increased dividends and forecasts of dividend rises frequently accompany profits revisions. During the protracted bid battle between *Consolidated Gold Fields* and *Minorco* in the first half of 1989, *Consolidated Gold Fields* pledged a special cash dividend of £6 gross per share if earnings per share of £4 over the following three years were not met. This novel announcement was christened a 'vitamin pill' in contrast to the more normal 'poison pills' that companies often employ (especially in the US) when subjected to a hostile bid.

More traditional is the response of *Ward White,* which raised its interim dividend by 20 per cent in response to the bid from *Boots* and predicted that its total dividend for the year would be 30 per cent higher than the previous year's. Along similar lines, the bid from *Sally Holdings* prompted *Red*

Funnel to raise its interim dividend by 50 per cent and its forecast of the total dividend for the year by 25 per cent.

In contrast, in conjunction with its reduced profits forecast, *Sketchley*'s response to the *Godfrey Davis* bid was to reduce its dividend from 20.9 pence per share to 13 pence.

Asset revaluations are particularly common among property companies, breweries and retail chains. For example, *Higgs and Hill* revalued its assets significantly in response to a bid from *Y J Lovell* in November 1989. The asset revaluation (which included an allowance for the value of future developments for which planning permission had not been obtained) valued the assets at 576 pence per share compared with an initial offer of 405 pence per share from *Lovell*. The offer was subsequently raised to 470 pence per share.

There are many other examples of asset revaluations being used as a defence tactic. During the course of a bid from *Peter Black Holdings* in April 1989, *Lambert Howarth Group* stated that a revaluation of its assets yielded a net asset value of 207 pence per share. This compared with an offer worth 165 pence per share at the time of the announcement of the bid from *Peter Black*.

Similarly, under threat from *Queens Moat Houses* in January 1990, *Norfolk Capital Group* commissioned a revaluation of its property portfolio. This valued *Norfolk*'s net assets at 53 pence per share and allowed it to claim that *Queens Moat* was undervaluing its assets by 24 per cent.

Finally, *Consolidated Gold Fields'* defence against the bid from *Hanson Trust* in June 1989 concentrated on the value of its subsidiary, ARC. The implied value of ARC from *Hanson*'s bid was £600 million in comparison with analysts' estimates of between £1.5 and £2.0 billion.

3.1.2 Corporate restructurings

There are three types of corporate restructuring: asset disposals, changes in management and management buy-outs.

Asset disposals: The most common form of corporate restructuring is the announcement by the target firm that parts of its existing business will be sold off. For example, the sale of subsidiaries, the disposal of holdings in other companies, the sale of specific assets, such as land or property, or the de-merging of completely separate businesses within a conglomerate can all be categorized as corporate restructurings.

The best known example of this occurred in the bid by *Hoylake* for *BAT* which began in July 1989. In September 1989, *BAT* announced a plan to slim the business into two activities, financial services and tobacco. Under the scheme, *BAT*'s paper-making activities and the *Argos* retail business were de-merged to form two new quoted companies in which *BAT* shareholders were offered shares. The remaining retailing and other interests were to be sold.

Along similar lines, part of *Hestair*'s defence against the *Adia Group* in September 1989 involved the sale of *Hestair Hope Limited* and *Hestair Kiddicraft*. It also planned to sell *McLaren* in the following year and become a pure employment agency.

Changes in management: It is noted above that executive changes often occur in anticipation of hostile bids. They can also occur during the course of a bid. One example of this was the resignation of *Sketchley*'s chairman on announcement of the *Compass* bid. Another example was the resignation of the managing director of *Molins* in *Leucadia National Corporation*'s bid for *Molins* in March 1990.

Management buy-outs: Management buy-outs came to prominence in the UK in the second half of the 1980s. In some cases they were management's response to hostile bids. *Marina Development*'s directors started working on a management buy-out proposal in response to a bid from the *Local London Group*, and *Ward White*'s management attempted a management buy-out in response to the bid from *Boots*.

3.1.3 White knights

A hostile bid puts the target company firmly 'in play'. The resultant attention in the press often attracts other potential bidders. In over 45 per cent of the hostile bids considered in this study further bidders entered the battle after the initial hostile bid. Clearly, such attention is not always welcomed by the target company, but when rival bidders appear whose bids are recommended by the target company, these are classified as white knights. Of course, it is quite possible that such white knights are more accurately viewed as the lesser of two evils. Few companies actually want to be taken over, and a company may recommend a rival bid only because it judges that, having been brought into play, some change in corporate control is inevitable.

Equally, in most cases, it is somewhat misleading to think of white knights as a takeover defence strategy by the incumbent management. First, few of the white knights in this study were actively encouraged by the target firm to mount a rival bid. Second, while a white knight may successfully defend the target company from the initial bid, in most cases the company is still taken over, albeit by the white knight. As mentioned above, even when the bids of white knights are recommended by the management of the target firm, this may be very much a second-best outcome for the incumbent management. If the roles had been reversed in the bid, with the white knight making the initial hostile bid, how many would have been accepted at that stage?

Consider, for example, the case of *Caparo Group*'s bid for *Armstrong Equipment* in September 1989. The day after the bid was announced *JH Fenner Holdings* raised its stake in *Armstrong* to 3.75 per cent and later to

6.3 per cent. It offered itself as a white knight. However, *Armstrong* wanted to remain independent and rejected the offer. *Fenner* eventually sold its stake to *Caparo*.

The case study that best exemplifies the phenomenon of the 'grey knight' is the series of bids for *Sketchley*. In the first bid for *Sketchley* from *Godfrey Davis*, *Compass* had been approached as a potential white knight by *Sketchley*. However, once the bid from *Godfrey Davis* had been rejected then a further approach from *Compass* was rejected by *Sketchley* and became a hostile bid of its own.

Along similar lines, *Meat Trade Suppliers* recommended a reverse take-over offer from *Alpha Gamma* after a bid from *Twigrealm* materialized. However, a previous proposal from *Alpha Gamma* for a reverse takeover had been rejected by the former chairman of the *Meat Trade Suppliers*.

One of the few true white knight defences during the period under consideration was *Omnicom*'s defence of *Boase Massimi Pollitt*. During the hostile bid from *Boulet Dru Dupuy Petit*, a privately owned French advertising agency, *Omnicom* made a rival bid for *BMP*, whose directors were offered positions in a new *Omnicom* UK subsidiary and on the main *Omnicom* board.

3.1.4 Poison pills

Poison pills have been employed in the US since 1985, when the Delaware Court upheld the legality of such arrangements. However, to date, they have been used relatively infrequently in the UK. As noted in Section 2.4 of Chapter 2, poison pills can take a variety of forms. In the US the most common poison pill is an arrangement whereby shareholders are issued with the right to preferred stock if a bid occurs (this is normally defined as a single shareholder acquiring more than, say, 30 per cent of the equity). These rights can be redeemed by the board of directors or exercised. If they are exercised, the resultant preferred stock might be convertible into ordinary shares at an extremely attractive price—essentially raising the cost of the bid. Such pills are referred to as 'flip-overs'. Alternatively, the rights might be repurchased by the issuing firm at a large premium over the issue price, with the large shareholder excluded from the repurchase. These are known as 'flip-ins'.

In the UK, poison pills have tended to take the form of granting certain options to existing management, and therefore should be described, more accurately, as 'golden parachutes'. For example, senior executives might be granted the option to resign on especially favourable terms in the event of a hostile bid, or share options might be exercisable in the event of a hostile bid which would, again, raise the cost of the takeover to the bidder. The important element of such defence tactics is that they favour the incumbent management, rather than the existing shareholders.

An example of the latter was revealed in the bid by *Meggitt* for *United Scientific Holdings*. The board of a US subsidiary announced that it had passed resolutions which allowed directors to receive £1.5 million in golden parachutes if control of *United Scientific* changed.

The directors of *Camford Engineering* had contracts which allowed them to resign with compensation for their five-year service contracts if any shareholding exceeded 30 per cent. *Markheath*, which was bidding for *Camford*, said that these contracts could cost £1.9 million in salaries.

While not strictly a poison pill defence, the management of a target company may have some ability to influence the structure of the shareholdings in the company without having a formal poison pill in place. For example, in the bid from *Local London Group*, *Marina Development Group* exercised options on 750 000 shares representing about 4.75 per cent of the company's capital. This had the effect of diluting *Local London*'s holdings from 47.7 per cent to 45.5 per cent.

3.1.5 Legal and/or political tactics

A variety of legal and political obstacles can be used to delay, or deter, a hostile bid. These include appeals to the Office of Fair Trading (including attempts to get the bid referred to the Monopolies and Mergers Commission); legal action in respect of possible violation of company law, in particular the Companies Act in the UK; claims that the bidder has broken the Takeover code; complaints to the Stock Exchange; and appeals to overseas authorities. In Table 3.3, we summarize the legal and/or political responses made by the companies in our sample.

There were attempts to get bids referred to the Monopolies Commission by *BAT*, *De La Rue*, *Dixons* and *Hartwell*. However, of these attempts, only *Dixons'* was successful.

There were complaints to courts about the use or misuse of information in the bids for *Marina Development*, *Norton Opax* and the *Ricardo Group*. There were complaints to the Takeover Panel about concert parties by *Goldberg*, *Metal Closures Group* and the *Tilbury Group*. The Stock Exchange was involved in bids for *Camford Engineering* and *Colonnade Development Capital* and there were representations to overseas regulators in the bid for *BAT* and *United Scientific Holdings*. Finally, *DRG* and *Pearl Assurance Group* used political lobbying.

3.2 BID BATTLES

A commonly held view is that the best protection against the threat of hostile bids is a strong financial record and a high share price. The standard description of the market for corporate control presented in Chapter 2 is

Table 3.3 Legal and political defences

Target	Bidder	Body to whom appeal was made	Nature of appeal
Bassett Foods	Procordia	Office of Fair Trading	Restrictions on access of British firms to Swedish stock market
BAT Industries	Hoylake	Office of Fair Trading; Takeover Panel; Securities and Exchange Commission; California Insurance Commissioner; and political	Various (see case)
De La Rue	Norton Opax	Office of Fair Trading	Monopoly
Dixons	Kingfisher	Office of Fair Trading; Political	Monopoly
Hartwell	Oakhill	Office of Fair Trading	Monopolies Commission reference for monopoly position
Marina Development	Local London Group	Courts	Misuse of confidential information
Ricardo Group	First Technology	Courts under the 1985 Companies Act	Inadequate information on beneficiaries
Gateway Corporation	Isosceles	Takeover Panel	Breach of rule forbidding increased offer
A. Goldberg & Sons	Blacks Leisure Group	Takeover Panel	Concert action
Metal Closures Group	Wassall	Takeover Panel	Concert action
Molins	Leucadia National	Takeover Panel	Creating confusion in the market
Norton Opax	Bowater Industries	Takover Panel and the Courts	Investment adviser party to privileged information
Tilbury Group	Lilley	Takeover Panel	Concert action
Ward White Group	Boots	Takeover Panel	Convertible preference shares should not be counted towards acceptances
Camford Engineering	Markheath Securities	Stock Exchange	Fair dealing between related entities
Colonnade Development Capital	Stratagem Group	Stock Exchange	Fair dealing between related entities
United Scientific Holdings	Meggitt	Singapore Securities Industry Council	Rules on minorities
DRG	Pembridge Investments	Political	Overseas bidder in tax haven
Pearl Assurance Group	Australian Mutual Provident	Political	Overseas bidder

that the takeover process targets poorly performing firms. As a consequence, firms devote considerable resources to the presentation of financial results and investor relations. In this section we examine this view of the takeover process in the light of the case studies.

3.2.1 Motives for bids

If the takeover process is to operate in a way that generates incentives for management to act in shareholder interests, a number of conditions should hold. First, firms that are performing relatively poorly should tend to be the subject of hostile bids. Second, if a hostile bid is launched for a firm that is performing well, there should be a high probability that the management can repel the bid. In other words, the 'managerial failure' view of hostile takeovers would predict that both the probability of a hostile bid occurring and the outcome of the bid should be influenced strongly by the pre-bid performance of the firm.

There is clearly no precise way of classifying whether a firm's performance has been poor prior to a bid taking place. Performance measures based on profitability figures are likely to be flawed for various reasons, including (i) the diversity of accounting conventions used in constructing profitability figures, in particular regarding exceptional items and valuations of assets; (ii) the absence of current cost accounts for most companies; (iii) the problem that profitability measures are inevitably backward-looking and include no estimate of future profitability, which may be of more relevance in the evaluation of management performance at any point in time.

Consequently, in this study we concentrate on indices of performance derived from equity market based measures, such as share price performance relative to the market, growth of earnings per share, and dividend performance. In particular, we classify the pre-bid performance of target companies according to whether there was:

- clear evidence of financial failure of the target in advance of the bid
- some evidence of financial failure on the part of the target, or
- no evidence of financial failure.

Clear evidence was deemed to be present when the share price of the target declined relative to the FT index in at least one of the two years prior to the bid *and* there was a decline in either earnings per share or dividends per share in the year immediately preceding the bid.

There was deemed to be *some evidence* of financial failure when there was *either* a decline in share prices relative to the market in at least one of the two years prior to the bid *or* a deterioration in earnings or dividends per share in the year immediately preceding the bid.

Firms were deemed to have demonstrated *no evidence* of financial failure where none of these events occurred.

Table 3.4 records the results of this classification. In 16 of the 42 bids there was clear evidence of financial failure; in 10 bids there was some evidence; and in 16 cases there was no evidence of financial failure. There was therefore at least some evidence of financial failure in over 60 per cent of cases.

In half of the cases where there was no evidence of financial failure, the hostile bid succeeded. In contrast, in only 37 per cent of cases where there was clear evidence of financial failure did bids succeed. The cases where there was the highest success rate of bids were those where there was some but not overwhelming evidence of financial failure.

How do we interpret the fact that in 40 per cent of the hostile bids in this sample there was no evidence—as captured by financial information—of failure prior to the bid? It should be recalled that takeover targets may not be selected by potential predators solely on the basis of poor financial performance. Various motives for takeovers exist apart from the opportunity to turn around a flagging company.

First, a number of bids appeared to be motivated by the strategic objectives of the raider. For instance, *Procordia* claimed that a successful takeover of *Bassett Foods* would allow it to pursue a policy of expansion into Europe. Without a sufficient product range the distribution and promotion costs of developing pan-European brands could not be justified. *Procordia* claimed that a takeover of *Bassett* would merge two complementary product lines and allow it to pursue its strategy of European expansion.

Second, there is often a belief on the part of the bidder that there are economies of scale to be earned from a takeover. For example, *Miss World Group* claimed during its attempted takeover of *Piccadilly Radio* that it would create the second largest radio group in the UK and produce a group with the sort of critical mass radio companies required to cope with the deregulation of the independent radio market. By combining the marketing and sales efforts of the two companies it was anticipated that significant cost savings could be achieved. Similar arguments were produced during the attempt by *Lovell* to take over *Higgs and Hill*. *Lovell* believed that significant economies of scale could be gained by combining two companies with complementary skills.

Finally, there are cases where, although the performance of the target has not been poor, the bidder claims that it could be improved. Of course, if such claims are correct the takeover target should really be categorized as having failed financially. A good example of such an attempted takeover was the protracted battle between *BAT* and *Hoylake*. The financial performance of *BAT* prior to the *Hoylake* bid had certainly not been poor: earnings per share had been rising steadily in each of the previous four years, and the *BAT* share price had risen significantly relative to the market index in the year prior to the bid.

Table 3.4 Bids classified by whether or not there was evidence of financial failure before the bid

Definite financial failure		Possible financial failure		No financial failure	
Target company	Bid success (S) or failure (F)	Target company	Bid success (S) or failure (F)	Target company	Bid success (S) or failure (F)
Lambert Howarth Group	F	Ricardo Group	F	Bassett Foods	F
Gateway Corporation	S	Boase Massimi Pollitt	F	Marina Development Group	F
Habitat Precision Engineering	S	Coalite Group	S	Chamberlain Phipps	F
Ketson	F	Consolidated Gold Fields	S	Local London Group	S
Molins	F	Ward White Group	S	Piccadilly Radio	S
A Goldberg & Sons	F	Armstrong Equipment	S	Red Funnel	F
De La Rue	F	Hestair	F	BAT Industries	F
Norton Opax	S	Metal Closures Group	S	Tilbury Group	F
United Scientific Holdings	F	Colonnade Development Capital	S	DRG	S
Meat Trade Suppliers	S	Molins	F	Pearl Assurance Group	S
Dixons	F			Higgs & Hill	F
Norfolk Capital Group	S			Hartwell	S
Sketchley (1)	F			Chemoxy International	F
Sketchley (2)	F			Laing Properties	S
Crystalate Holdings	S			Walter Runciman	S
				Camford Engineering	S
Total number 16		Total number 10		Total number 16	
Successful bids 6		Successful bids 6		Successful bids 8	
Failed bids 10		Failed bids 4		Failed bids 8	

Yet *Hoylake* claimed that significantly greater returns for shareholders could be gained by changing the management strategy and 'unbundling' the various component businesses of *BAT*. In the event the bid failed but *Hoylake*'s claim was borne out by the subsequent decision of the *BAT* management to mimic the *Hoylake* strategy and sell off various businesses within the group, such as the *Argos* retailing operation. As a result the 'takeover premium' did not disappear when the *Hoylake* bid failed, and shareholders have enjoyed significant gains.

This last case is an example of the role hostile takeover bids can play in initiating wholesale changes in corporate strategy. It has often been claimed that once businesses become very large it is very difficult, in practice, for the incumbent management to introduce a radically new strategy. For example, there was a trend towards the creation of conglomerates in the 1980s, with diverse businesses being bundled together. One justification for such a strategy was that by combining different businesses within a conglomerate, the group would not be overly dependent upon the performance of any one business, and so a less volatile earnings stream and share price would result.

These particular arguments in favour of building a conglomerate business are, of course, very weak. Shareholders are able to diversify risks themselves by holding the shares of many different companies in their portfolios; they do not need the management of any individual company to perform this task for them. As a result, in recent years there has been a de-merger boom in both the US and the UK. In the US such restructuring was often achieved via a leveraged hostile bid for the conglomerate. By selling off component businesses the bidders could then gradually reduce their leverage and increase the value of the remaining core business. Many have claimed that without a hostile takeover the inertia that exists within many large organizations would have prevented such efficiency-enhancing (and shareholder value-enhancing) restructurings from taking place.

The discussion in this section should demonstrate an important point: that takeovers need not be motivated solely by management failure. The evidence presented above, and in the case studies in the second part of the book, suggests that simply managing the company well is not a reliable defence against a hostile bid: there is little relation between the financial performance of a target before acquisition and either the likelihood of a hostile bid emerging or the outcome of that bid. This is, perhaps, a worrying aspect of hostile takeovers; namely that they do not necessarily produce appropriate incentive structures for management and that, as a result, corporate performance may in some cases be adversely affected.

In the next section we examine how target firms respond to hostile bids.

3.2.2 Defence tactics

Following the classification introduced earlier in this chapter, the various defence tactics used by target firms have been grouped into five categories: financial responses, corporate restructurings, poison pills, white knights, and legal and/or political tactics. The types of financial response are broken down further into dividend announcements, profit announcements, asset announcements and other types of financial response. A summary of the defence tactics used is presented in Table 3.5. As can be seen, most firms use multiple defences, and two of the firms in the sample produced no response that we would classify as a formal defence tactic.

It is no surprise that most takeover targets which reject an initial bid make some form of financial response: in our sample over 80 per cent of target firms produced some form of financial response. Figure. 3.1 shows the proportion of bids in which the target used each type of defence tactic. The percentages add up to nearly 200 per cent, reflecting the fact that, on average, firms tend to employ about 2 different types of defence.

It is perhaps surprising that around 45 per cent of the takeover targets attempted to use some form of legal and/or political defence. White knights—rival bidders whose bids were recommended by the target management—emerged in 31 per cent of the bids. Corporate restructurings were announced in around 21 per cent of cases and various forms of poison pills were used, or were attempted, in 12 per cent of the bids.

If we consider the different types of financial response, dividend and profits announcements emerge as the typical form of response. As can be

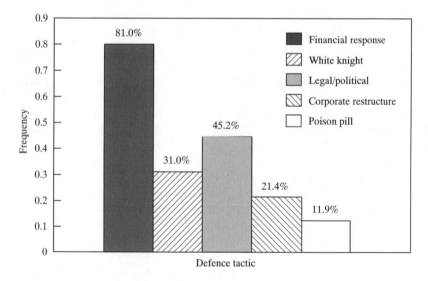

Figure 3.1 Frequency of different defence tactics

Table 3.5 Defence tactics used

Target	Defence tactic employed*					Type of financial response†			
	FR	WK	LP	CR	PP	D	P	A	O
Bassett Foods		•	•						
Ricardo Group	•	•				•	•		
Marina Development Group		•	•	•	•				
Chamberlain Phipps		•							
Local London Group									
Boase Massimi Pollitt	•	•				•	•		
Lambert Howarth Group	•					•	•	•	
Piccadilly Radio									
Gateway Corporation	•	•	•			•	•	•	
Habit Precision Engineering	•						•		
Ketson	•								•
Coalite Group	•					•	•		
Business Mortgages Trust	•	•				•	•		
Molins	•					•	•	•	•
Consolidated Gold Fields	•								•
Red Funnel	•	•				•	•		
Ward White Group	•		•	•		•	•		
BAT Industries	•		•	•		•	•		
Tilbury Group	•		•			•	•	•	
A Goldberg & Sons	•	•	•				•		
De La Rue			•						
Norton Opax	•		•						•
United Scientific Holdings	•		•	•	•			•	
Armstrong Equipment		•			•				
Meat Trade Suppliers	•								
DRG	•		•			•	•		
Pearl Assurance Group	•		•			•		•	
Higgs & Hill	•					•	•		•
Hestair	•	•		•					•
Metal Closures Group	•		•			•	•		
Dixons	•		•			•	•		
Colonnade Development Capital	•		•	•		•		•	
Hartwell	•		•			•	•	•	
Norfolk Capital Group	•			•				•	
Chemoxy International	•	•						•	•
Laing Properties	•					•	•	•	
Sketchley (1)	•					•	•		
Walter Runciman	•		•			•	•		
Camford Engineering	•	•		•		•	•	•	
Sketchley (2)	•				•		•		
Molins	•		•	•					•
Crystalate Holdings	•	•					•		

Defences: FR = financial response, WK = white knight, LP = legal and/or political, CR = corporate restructure, PP = poison pill.
†*Financial responses*: D = dividend, P = profit, A = assets, O = other.

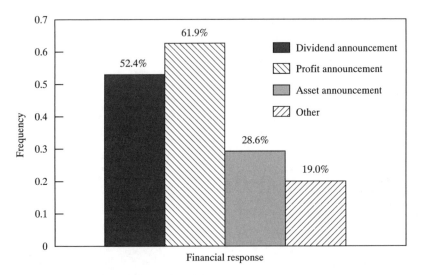

Figure 3.2 Frequency of different financial responses

seen in Fig. 3.2, the majority of firms made both dividend and profit announcements. In almost all cases these constitute more optimistic forecasts than had hitherto been made, although in the two bids for *Sketchley* and the bid for *United Scientific* the companies announced reduced profits and/or dividends.

Asset announcements were used rather less frequently, by around 29 per cent of takeover targets. These typically involved the sale of assets at above previous estimates of their value, or the revaluation of existing assets. A variety of financial responses that do not fit into the other categories are included in 'other'. Examples include *Higgs & Hill* which announced that it had won a lucrative new contract during the battle with *Lovell*, and *Molins* which predicted that revenue would increase significantly if litigation in the US was successful.

3.3 BID OUTCOMES

3.3.1 The value of defence

All the bids considered in this book are hostile, that is, they were initially rejected by the incumbent management. In practice, there are two types of hostile bid. First, two companies may have been talking about a possible merger, but fail to agree on terms. One company then launches a bid for the other. Such advances are normally rejected by the target management, even though the potential merits of the two companies merging may have already been established. Second, one company may make a bid for another company without having entered into any prior negotiations or discussions. Typically a company will discover it is a target when the chairman or chief executive receives an early morning phone call from the bidder informing them that a bid is about to be launched. It is almost unheard of for the incumbent management not to initially reject such offers. But is this in the interests of shareholders?

There are, of course, good and bad reasons for management to mount a takeover defence. The bad reasons—at least from the point of view of the shareholders—revolve around the natural desire of incumbent management to keep their jobs. Being taken over is often interpreted as a sign of the failure of the existing managers: the bidder, by offering a bid premium, is indicating that it could make better use of the firm's resources, and so increase the value of the firm. There are certainly cases when existing management has failed, and it would be better for the shareholders if they were replaced. However, there are cases when a vigorous defence of a bid is in the interests of both the management and the shareholders of the target company.

The most obvious case for the defence is that, by rejecting an initial hostile bid, a higher offer can be encouraged. By mounting a vigorous defence, a better price may be achieved. Of course, this may be the case irrespective of whether the existing management has failed. This is reflected in the case studies reported in Part 2: in only 2 of the 42 bids did the target not mount some significant form of defence.

A related argument for the defence is that the bid may fail to take account of the assets and future prospects of the firm. In a large number of cases, target management claim that the bidder is attempting to 'buy the company on the cheap'. This may well be the case. Few firms announce their entire corporate strategy and prospects to the outside world, and the managers of the target firm may well have privileged information which, if released, would increase the market value of the firm. Of course, to mount a defence on such grounds, it is necessary to reveal such private information—some of which may be commercially sensitive—and allow their shareholders, and the market, to evaluate its worth. By mounting such a defence, management may be able to increase the market value of the target firm to such an extent that the bid fails, or, even if the bid succeeds, secure a higher price for their shareholders.

3.3.2 Success and failure

Table 3.6 summarizes the outcomes of the bids considered in this study. We report not only whether the bid was successful or failed but also whether the initial bid was revised in the course of the battle. Twenty-three of the

Table 3.6 Bid Outcomes

Target	Bidder	Bid failed	Higher offer
Bassett Foods	Procordia A.B. (Sweden)	Y	N
Ricardo Group	First Technology	Y	Y
Marina Development Group	Local London Group	Y	N
Chamberlain Phipps	Bowater Industries	Y	Y
Local London Group	Priest Marians Holdings	N	N
Boase Massimi Pollitt	Boulet Dru Dupuy Petit	Y	Y
Lambert Howarth Group	Peter Black Holdings	Y	Y
Piccadilly Radio	Miss World Group	N	Y
Gateway Corporation	Isosceles	N	Y
Habit Precision Engineering	Epicure Holdings	N	Y
Ketson	Moneytab	Y	N
Coalite Group	Anglo United	N	Y
Business Mortgages Trust	National Home Loans	Y	N
Molins	IEP Securities	Y	Y
Consolidated Gold Fields	Hanson Trust	N	Y
Red Funnel	Sally Holdings UK	Y	Y
Ward White Group	Boots	N	Y
BAT Industries	Hoylake	Y	N
Tilbury Group	Lilley	Y	Y
A Goldberg & Sons	Blacks Leisure Group	Y	N
De La Rue	Norton Opax	Y	Y
Norton Opax	Bowater Industries	N	N
United Scientific Holdings	Meggitt	Y	N
Armstrong Equipment	Caparo Group	N	Y
Meat Trade Suppliers	Twigrealm	N	N
DRG	Pembridge Investments	N	N
Pearl Assurance Group	Australian Mutual Provident	N	Y
Higgs & Hill	Y J Lovell	Y	Y
Hestair	Adia Group (Switzerland)	Y	N
Metal Closures Group	Wassall	N	N
Dixons	Kingfisher	Y	N
Colonnade Development Capital	Stratagem Group	N	Y
Hartwell	Oakhill	Y	Y
Norfolk Capital Group	Queens Moat Houses	N	N
Chemoxy International	MTM	Y	N
Laing Properties	Pall Mall Properties	N	Y
Sketchley (1)	Godfrey Davis	Y	N
Walter Runciman	Forvaltnings Avena (Sweden)	N	Y
Camford Engineering	Markheath Securities	N	Y
Sketchley (2)	Compass Group	Y	N
Molins	Leucadia National Corporation (US)	Y	Y
Crystalate Holdings	TT Group	N	N

forty-two bids failed. As reported in Chapter 1, over the period 1984–89 around 45 per cent of hostile bids were unsuccessful, and so our sample has a slightly higher proportion of unsuccessful bids than the average observed in recent years. Just over half of the bids were increased at some stage during the bid battle, providing justification for incumbent management rejection of the initial bids.

In Table 3.7 we analyse the outcomes of the bids in more detail. Bids are categorized according to their success or failure and also according to whether the initial bid was increased or not. If an initial offer fails, and no higher offer is made, the outcome is classified as 'initial offer failed'. If an initial offer is increased during the bid battle, but the bid is still unsuccessful, the bid is classified as 'higher offer failed'. Similarly, if the initial bid is accepted by shareholders, the bid is classified as 'initial offer succeeded', whereas if an initial bid is increased during the takeover battle, and the bid is successful, the outcome is classified as 'higher offer succeeded'.

Table 3.7 also classifies bids by the means of payment used: 43 per cent of bids were for cash, 21 per cent were for equity and 36 per cent were for a mixture of equity and debt. There are some noticeable differences in the success rate of different means of payment: nearly 56 per cent of cash bids succeeded, whereas only 11 per cent of bids which offered only shares were ultimately successful; 53 per cent of all mixed cash/equity bids succeeded.

There are interesting patterns in terms of the bidder's strategy during the bid battle: 78 per cent of initial equity bids were *not* increased, while nearly 67 per cent of cash bids were increased in the course of the bid, and of these over 58 per cent were successful. It appears that shareholders expect initial cash bids to be increased during the bid battle; this may affect the price the bidder initially offers and the reaction of shareholders or target management to the initial bid. One of the consequences of the differences in the frequency of revision of bids is that bid premiums are higher in cash financed acquisitions (around 35 per cent on average in this sample) than in equity or mixed bids (around 26 per cent on average).

Table 3.7 Bid outcomes and methods of payment

	Initial offer failed	Higher offer failed	Initial offer succeeded	Higher offer succeeded	Total
Cash	17%	28%	17%	39%	18
Shares	67%	22%	11%	0%	9
Cash and shares	27%	20%	20%	33%	15
All bids	31%	24%	17%	29%	42

3.3.3 The success of defence strategies

At first sight, this evidence might suggest that there is very little relation between success of defence and the type of defence employed. Figure 3.3 illustrates the success rate of different defence tactics. It suggests that the success rate is rather similar for different defences.

However, on closer inspection a very clear pattern begins to emerge. A distinction needs to be drawn between four different classes of bid: cash bids where a white knight appeared; cash bids where there was no white knight; equity or mixed bids with a strong defence by the target; and equity or mixed bids with a weak defence (Fig. 3.4).

The first question that arises is whether the bid was for cash. If so, did a white knight emerge? Where another bidder entered the battle, in the sample of firms in this study, its bid was always recommended by the target firm and was therefore classified as a white knight. If there is more than one bidder then the contest becomes one between the two bidders, and the actions of the target, save that of recommending one of the bids, are of comparatively little relevance.

If the bid was not for cash i.e. if it was for equity or was a mixed bid) then the second question is what was the nature of the target's defence. In the absence of a white knight, the defence of the target becomes of crucial importance.

Finally, two special cases not considered above are, firstly, that the bidder withdrew and, secondly, that a regulatory body intervened to prevent the bid proceeding.

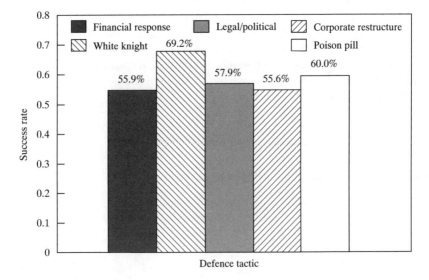

Figure 3.3 Success rate of different defence strategies

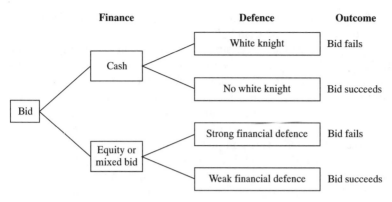

Figure 3.4 Determinants of bid outcomes

Table 3.8 records that where a white knight entered, bids almost invariably failed. One of the two cases where the bid still succeeded was *Meat Trade Suppliers*. The white knight bid by *Alpha Gamma* was only partial (i.e. for a portion, not all of the shares of *Meat Trade Suppliers*). The one genuine case where the white knight failed to secure the bid was the takeover of *Gateway* by *Isosceles*. The intervention by *Newgateway* failed despite being a cash offer. The unusual feature of this bid was the constraints imposed on the rivals by the ways in which the bids were financed.

Bid premiums tend to be higher in bids where a white knight emerges. The average bid premium in cases where there was a white knight was around 41 per cent compared with an average of around 29 per cent where there was no white knight. In part this is associated with the higher bid premiums observed in cash bids than in equity or mixed bids noted above. Seven out of nine of the cases of white knights reported in Table 3.8 were cash bids. The two cases where the bids were not for cash failed to go through.

Where no white knight emerges then cash offers almost invariably succeed. In some cases (e.g. *Coalite Group*, *DRG*, *Walter Runciman*, and

Table 3.8 Main determinants of the outcome of bids

	Cases of white knight intervention*	No white knight			
		Cash offer	Equity of mixed offer	Regulatory intervention	Bidder withdrew
Successful bids	2	12	5	N/A	N/A
Failed bids	7	2	7	3	4

*There were two cases where white knights failed to bid: one case where a bid was withdrawn, and one case where the action of the Monopolies Commission prevented the white knight from succeeding.

Camford Engineering) cash offers succeeded in the face of strong defences by targets. Both the cases where cash bids failed to go through involved bids for the same company—*Molins*. The success of *Molins* in remaining independent in the face of cash offers appears to have been intimately associated with the loyalty of one large dominant shareholder.

In contrast, where there is no white knight, equity or mixed offers succeed and fail in about equal proportions. Table 3.9 suggests that the nature of the defence put up by the target is of crucial importance in the case of non-cash bids. The cases where bids were completed seem to have involved very weak defences. In one case there was disarray in the target's board; in another, there was a deterioration in profits during the bid. At best, these weak defences simply comprised improved profit projections. Even in the case where the board was in disarray, the bid only just succeeded.

In contrast, firms that successfully defended themselves announced profits and dividends increases and, in particular, revealed asset valuations that suggested that targets were undervalued by raiders. In the cases of *Lambert Howarth Group*, *Tilbury* and *Higgs and Hill* asset revaluations succeeded in overturning takeovers with large bid premiums. The case of *Sketchley* was unusual in announcing a profit reduction because this had previously been successful in causing *Godfrey Davis* to withdraw.

There may be some relation between the ability of firms to defend themselves in equity and mixed offer bids and their performance in advance of a bid. In most cases, where there is a weak defence of equity bids, there is at least some evidence of financial failure. However, the presence of financial

Table 3.9 Defences employed by targets of equity of mixed offers where there was no white knight

Target	Defence
Successful defences	
Ricardo Group	Profits and dividends increases
Lambert Howarth Group	Profits and dividends increases
Ketson	Threat to rights issue (other financial)
Tilbury Group	Asset valuation
A Goldberg & Sons	Uncertainty about valuation of bidder's equity
Higgs and Hill	Asset valuation
Sketchley (twice)	Downward revision to profits
Unsuccessful defences	
Piccadilly Radio	None, although there was a limitation on voting rights in place
Habit Precision Engineering	Profit projections
Norton Opax	Profit projections
Metal Closures Group	(Reduced profits revealed during bid)
Norfolk Capital Group	(Diversities revealed among the board)

failure is not sufficient to ensure the success of an equity or mixed bid. *Lambert Howarth Group, Ketson, Goldberg* and *Sketchley* were able to repel bids despite displaying clear evidence of financial failure in advance of a bid.

Finally, to return to Table 3.8, we see that in the remaining cases bidders either withdrew or regulatory intervention was effective. There were four cases where the bidder withdrew. Two bidders (*Local London Group* and *Norton*) withdrew because of dissident shareholders (*Brent Walker* and *Bowater* respectively) who proceeded to support or launch bids against the raider. The other two cases of bidder withdrawal occurred when it became apparent that the raider had overbid (*Meggitt's* bid for *United Scientific Holdings* and *Godfrey Davis'* bid for *Sketchley*).

As noted above, appeals to regulatory bodies and the courts are very common. In a large majority of cases these are completely ineffective or at best merely an irritant to the bidder. There were just three cases in this analysis where regulatory intervention really proved decisive: the bids for *BAT, Dixons* and *Crystalate Holdings*. The bid by *Hoylake* for *BAT* was blocked by the California Insurance Commissioner who refused to approve the change of ownership of *Farmers Insurance* (a subsidiary of *BAT*). The bid by *Kingfisher* for *Dixons* was referred to the Monopolies and Mergers Commission which blocked the bid. Finally, in the case of the battle for *Crystalate Holdings*, the white knight bid by *Vishay* was referred to the MMC, which was a decisive factor in the eventual success of the original bidder *TT Group*.

3.4 SUMMARY

This chapter has recorded a wide array of defences employed by targets of hostile bids. These have been classified as financial responses, corporate restructurings, poison pills, white knights, and legal/political tactics. Of these, financial responses were the most common and poison pills the least common. Most financial responses involve dividend and profit announcements.

This chapter reports only a weak relation between the pre-bid financial performance of targets and either the emergence of a hostile bid or the likelihood of success. In 40 per cent of bids there was no evidence of financial failure prior to the bid. In half the cases where there was no evidence of financial failure the hostile bid still succeeded. In contrast, in only 37 per cent of cases where there was clear evidence of financial failure did bids succeed. Several motives other than past financial failure appear to prompt hostile bids. These include: (i) strategic objectives, for instance a desire by predators to expand into new markets, and (ii) expectations on the

part of predators that performance can be improved by exploiting economies of scale or synergies or by introducing new management even though
financial failure has not occurred in the past.

Whatever the motives for a hostile bid, this study suggests that when firms
are subject to cash bids then unless they find white knights they almost
inevitably face defeat. When they are presented with equity or mixed offers
then spirited defences are frequently effective even where there is evidence of
financial failure before the bid. In particular, attacking the performance of
the bidder is often an effective defence in the case of bids with an equity
component. This is not surprising since the value of the bid to the shareholders of the target firm will depend, at least in part, on the market value of
the bidder's shares. By drawing attention to weaknesses in a bidder's management, accounting policy, past performance, or overall corporate strategy,
the target company can often turn the attention of the financial markets
away from itself and onto the bidder, frequently with depressing effects on
the latter's share price.

Of course, such tactics are unlikely to be effective in the case of cash bids,
and this is indeed what the case studies show. Since the shareholders in the
target firm will not be paid in shares, they should be entirely uninterested in
either the past or the prospective performance of the bidder, whose cash is as
good as anyone else's! As this study has demonstrated, shareholders invariably accept hostile bids made for cash, and so the only effective 'defence' is
the introduction of another bidder (perhaps with the support of the incumbent target management) to propose a higher cash offer. In these cases the
original hostile bid is often repelled, but control of the company still invariably changes.

The other tactic frequently employed by firms is that of various legal and/
or political defences. Despite the frequency with which these are employed,
in only a few cases are appeals to regulatory bodies decisive. Their main
effect is often to delay proceedings and, in all likelihood, to increase the
costs of the bid to both the bidder and the target.

4

CONCLUSIONS AND IMPLICATIONS

One of the most valuable results of a detailed analysis of case studies of hostile takeovers is that clear patterns can be revealed. As will become apparent from the second part of this book, despite the fact that the management of virtually all target companies attempt to defend themselves against a hostile bid in a spirited—and no doubt costly—manner, when the bid is for cash the only effective defence for UK companies appears to be finding a white knight. However, white knights are rarely desirable in themselves; they are often the lesser of two evils. Even if the management of target firms are able to retain their jobs (and this is frequently not the case), control is generally ceded to the acquiring firm. This is shown by the high level of restructurings of targets of unsuccessful bids noted in Chapter 1.

Of course, there may be criteria other than retaining control that motivate the target management during the battle. For instance, strong financial responses, such as revised profits forecasts or asset revaluations, may succeed in raising the price paid by the bidder. Such defence will clearly be in the interests of the target's shareholders, although the same cannot be true of all defence tactics (such as appeals to regulatory authorities).

This general conclusion—that when a hostile bid for cash is made, control of the company invariably changes (either to the bidder or a white knight)—appears to hold true irrespective of the pre-bid financial performance of the target company. As many companies in our sample became the subject of a hostile bid after a period of strong financial performance (as measured by share price performance, dividend growth and earnings per share) as those that had recorded very weak financial performance in the year preceding the bid. Furthermore, there was little difference in the success rates of hostile bids according to the pre-bid performance of the target companies in our sample. Such evidence calls into question the maxim 'the best takeover defence is running the company well'.

Somewhat in contrast, where bids are not for cash, spirited financial responses appear more effective. In addition, when the bidder is offering its shares as payment (at least in part) then a whole new set of takeover defences become available: attacking the bidder. Such tactics are of limited, if any, use in the case of a cash bid, since the past performance, future prospects or any other features of the bidder are unlikely to be of any relevance to the target shareholder in deciding whether to accept the cash of the bidder.

In practice, therefore, the case studies suggest that the managers of UK companies are extremely vulnerable to a hostile bid, with few effective defences available to them. However, we would go further and claim that compared to the management of companies in other major economies UK managers are uniquely vulnerable. This appears to be the case not only relative to the more 'bank-based' financial systems of Germany, Japan and most other European countries, but also relative to the superficially similar financial system of the US. As Chapter 2 demonstrated, US companies have a wide variety of takeover defences available to them under existing corporate law and financial regulation that would be impossible to implement in the UK (such as most forms of poison pill). Furthermore, in many cases the US defences seem extremely effective, either in raising significantly the cost of mounting a hostile bid or in preventing the possibility of a successful hostile bid entirely.

This raises a substantive policy issue: should UK companies be able to erect more substantial or effective barriers to hostile acquisition, and what impediments currently prevent companies implementing such defences? We conclude Part 1 of this book by suggesting some answers to these controversial issues.

The former question is inevitably highly contentious. It is similar in form to the issue of whether academics should have security of tenure, or for how long a politician should be elected. Protect a manager from a hostile bid and he or she may cease to pursue the interests of the shareholders so vigorously, claims one school of thought. But managers who constantly live under the threat of removal may discount the long-term future performance of the company at a higher rate than a manager with a more secure tenure. Why initiate long-term projects whose fruit may be enjoyed by others? In a world in which employment contracts could be written in a theoretically 'perfect' way—to include all contingencies and where the contribution of a particular individual to the company could be accurately and objectively valued at all points in time—such issues might be less important. But fundamental informational problems result in highly incomplete employment contracts for managers in practice, with partial attempts to remunerate the ousted manager—such as golden parachutes—being very much an imperfect solution to a very real problem.

We suggest that there should be no presumption that unfettered markets for corporate control are always appropriate. Managers should be given incentives to be efficient in both a *static* and a *dynamic* sense. Static efficiency would require managers to minimize costs, and earn the highest current rate of return for shareholders given the capital stock of the firm. Dynamic efficiency would require the managers to pursue investment policies that maximize long-term shareholder value.

A constant threat of hostile acquisition is likely to encourage static efficiency, but it should be recalled that companies in other economies (such as Japan or Germany) appear to achieve such efficiency quite well without any such threat. This is not surprising given that numerous other spurs to static efficiency exist, for example active product market competition, the personal motivation of managers, performance-related remuneration or monitoring by other investors or market analysts, to name but a few.

But we have suggested that dynamic efficiency may be impaired by the threat of a hostile bid, and that certain companies—perhaps those with large R&D expenditures or other long-term investments—should be able to erect some limited technical defences to takeover (despite the fact that EC harmonization proposals would, if ever implemented, tend to limit such defences).

However, in the case of UK companies we believe that such defences should have two key features:

- they should be implemented only with the agreement of shareholders
- they should be of limited duration and subject to review at an Annual General Meeting.

The first condition would rule out defences employed by managers that would clearly reduce the wealth of shareholders ('greenmail' as used in the US is probably the leading example of such a defence). The managers would be required to make a case for additional protection, and would, perhaps, be encouraged to present final and intermediate financial targets for the company over the period of protection against which they would ultimately be judged. If shareholders thought that, balancing the static versus dynamic efficiency arguments, it was in their interests to protect their managers, they would approve such a proposal. The evidence from the US is that shareholders will frequently approve measures such as anti-takeover charter amendments or, indeed, poison pills, when asked.

The second condition—the limited time duration of the takeover defences—would prevent managers becoming too entrenched. At the time of the review shareholders would have to evaluate the performance of the managers and decide whether the promised benefits had been forthcoming. If they had been disappointed, protection could be removed, or perhaps suspended, at which point the free market for corporate control would be re-established.

Such shareholder-approved limited-time protection seems the most appropriate response given the institutional features of the UK. It would be a mistake, we believe, to look overseas at the existing alternative systems of corporate control and attempt to superimpose such systems onto the UK, when the appropriate institutions do not exist or the regulatory and legal framework is quite different. For example, suggesting that banks should play a more active role in controlling companies (along the lines of the German model) seems quite inappropriate in the UK where banks have traditionally neither been providers of equity finance nor held proxy voting rights (due to the absence of bearer shares in the UK), and where bankers have not traditionally served on boards of directors (which is not surprising given the unitary boards of UK companies in comparison to the two-tier boards of most German companies), and where the majority of bankers have viewed their role quite narrowly as providers of finance and financial services rather than in controlling companies.

Would the implementation of the takeover defences we have discussed require changes in legislation? Obviously, the answer depends on what form the takeover defences took. But there are various defences which do not seem to be ruled out at present under the company law and securities regulation. For instance, we know of no formal impediment to the equivalent of US charter amendment (that is, changes in a company's articles of association), provided the required proportion of the shareholders agree at the appropriate general meeting. As described in Chapter 2, such amendments can be very effective at deterring a bid, and include super-majority clauses, and limitations on the number of votes that can be cast by any one shareholder. Along rather different lines, cross-shareholding arrangements are clearly possible (given that a number of UK companies have already entered into them). On the other hand, most forms of poison pill defence would not be possible in the UK, as they frequently violate the pre-emption rights of shareholders.

However, while it would appear that management already have the ability to propose to their shareholders various forms of takeover protection, we are less optimistic regarding the response they would receive. The rights of the shareholder to receive bids from alternative bidders, and ultimately to decide who runs the company, seem jealously guarded in certain quarters in the UK. The type of takeover protection we outline above still allows shareholders the ultimate power to decide whether such protection is appropriate and if it should be renewed once implemented. As such it would represent a very limited, yet potentially significant, relinquishment of power by shareholders.

It may be, of course, that there is something peculiar about the UK manager which results in optimal long-term performance being achieved only if he or she constantly faces the threat of replacement. Alternatively, it may be that the UK system of corporate control is optimal and provides a significant advantage to industry over the systems operating in other major economies (which provide considerably more protection to the incumbent management). However, the debate over corporate governance and control has been raging long enough in the UK to suggest that some alternative approaches should be considered and that, for some companies, there might be value in a self-denying ordinance on the part of shareholders.

Appendix 1

REFERENCES

Booz Allen (1989), *Obstacles to Takeover Bids in the European Community*, London.

Coopers & Lybrand (1989), *Barriers to Takeover in the European Community*, Report to the Department of Trade and Industry, HMSO, London.

Dann, L.Y. and H. DeAngelo (1983), 'Standstill agreements, privately negotiated stock repurchases and the market for corporate control', *Journal of Financial Economics*, **11**, No. 1, pp. 275–300.

Franks, J. and C. Mayer (1990), 'Capital markets and corporate control: a study of France, Germany and the UK', *Economic Policy*, **10**, No. 1, pp. 189–231.

Franks, J. and C. Mayer (1991), *Takeovers and the Correction of Managerial Failure*, London Business School Working Paper.

G.A. Jarrell and A.B. Poulsen (1987), 'Shark repellents and stock prices: the effect of anti-takeover amendments since 1980', *Journal of Financial Economics*, **19**, No. 1, pp. 127–168.

Jensen, M. and R. Ruback (1983), 'The market for corporate control: the scientific evidence', *Journal of Financial Economics*, **11**, No. 1, pp. 5–50.

Kester, W.C. (1992), 'Industrial groups as systems of contractual governance,' *Oxford Review of Economic Policy*, **8**, pp. 24–44.

Linn S.C. and J.J. McConnell (1983), 'An empirical investigation of the impact of "anti-take-over" charter amendments on common stock prices', *Journal of Financial Economics*, **11**, No. 1, pp. 361–399.

PART TWO
CASE STUDIES

HOSTILE TAKEOVERS—DETAILED CASES

CASE STUDY 1: BASSETT FOODS

Target: Bassett Foods

Sale of sugar confectionery in the UK, the US and the Netherlands. Brands include Liquorice Allsorts and Jelly Babies.

Bidder: Procordia A.B. (Sweden)

Consumer goods (beer, soft drinks, confectionery, tobacco), services (hotels and security), pharmaceuticals and engineering. Quoted on the Stockholm Stock Exchange with a state ownership of about 81 per cent.

> **Announcement:** 12 January 1989
> **Value of bid:** £60.0m
> **Defences:** White Knight, legal and/or political
> **Outcome:** BID FAILED

Summary

Bassett intended to appeal to the Office of Fair Trading about the access restrictions faced by British companies wishing to acquire Swedish companies.

Bassett then recommended a domestic counter-bid from Cadbury at a premium to Procordia's offer.

Background

Bassett was the only quoted company of significant size operating mainly in the sugar confectionery market. It commanded 11 per cent of the UK sugar confectionery market, putting it in third place behind Trebor with 15 per cent and Rowntree with 12 per cent. Bassett had invested heavily in rebuilding several of its brands in the UK and was developing a market in the Netherlands through a recent acquisition. In October 1988 Bassett bought Jamesons Chocolate for £8.74m.

The UK market for sugar confectionery, which was worth about £1 billion a year, was fragmented and undergoing rationalization. Large-scale restructuring of the chocolate confectionery market in the UK and on the continent had driven down unit costs and facilitated heavy promotion spending on brands. The sugar confectionery industry, with a proliferation of family companies, had by contrast much lower profit margins and hence less money to invest in building brands.

Procordia had 12 per cent of its domestic sugar confectionery market and was seeking international representation. It claimed that changes in the highly fragmented European sugar confectionery market would accelerate after 1992. Satellite broadcasting would change the nature of the market and a sufficient product range was needed to justify the distribution and promotion costs required to service it and develop pan-European brands. Procordia said the two companies had complementary product lines and it offered to provide Bassett with marketing expertise and financial resources for expansion.

Procordia's cash offer of 400p a share valued Bassett at about £63m on a multiple of 21.3. The shares closed at 455p, up 156p in two days. There was also a loan note alternative. Procordia had accumulated 10.1 per cent of Bassett's share capital before the bid. Bassett claimed the offer was at a 'bargain basement price' and it was capable of independent expansion.

Defence

WHITE KNIGHT On 2 February 1989 Cadbury Schweppes made a recommended offer for Bassett on the basis of 8 new Cadbury shares for every 5 already held in Bassett—the equivalent of 579p a share. The offer valued Bassett at £91m and had a cash alternative of 536p. Cadbury amassed 14.9 per cent of Bassett's shares in the market. Cadbury claimed Bassett would suit its long-term aim to expand its presence in the sugar confectionery market. The combined group would command 15 per cent of the UK sugar confectionery market. Management control of the combined group's sugar confectionery business was to pass entirely to Bassett.

LEGAL AND/OR POLITICAL Bassett also made a submission to the Office of Fair Trading. It argued that Procordia should not be allowed to acquire Bassett as British companies do not have reciprocal access to the Swedish market. In Sweden, an Act on Foreign Acquisitions decrees that the government must grant permission for a foreign company to buy 10 per cent of a Swedish company's votes or capital. Additional approval is required to breach the 20, 30, 40 and ultimately 50 per cent thresholds. Swedish companies also have a share structure divided between 'free' and 'restricted' shares which curtails foreign ownership. Bassett made its submission to the OFT public even after the white knight emerged. Its case was based on arguments similar to those made by Rowntree in seeking protection against the bid from Nestlé when Lord Young, the Trade and Industry secretary, said the bidder's ownership structure was irrelevant and that impact on competition in the UK was the key criterion.

Outcome

After the white knight emerged Procordia extended its bid to 22 February 1989. At the second close Procordia allowed its bid to lapse and subsequently reduced its holding to 6.7 per cent. Cadbury's recommended offer was declared unconditional in all respects on 4 March 1989 after valid acceptances had been received in respect of 72.1 per cent of Bassett's shares including the 14.9 per cent stake held by Cadbury. Holders of 19.8 per cent of the shares opted for the cash alternative.

Table CS1.1 Financial performance of Bassett Foods plc, 1978–1988

A/c year ending	Div per share	Net eps (adjusted)	p/e ratio*	p/e ratio (sector)†
1978	5.73	19.67	10.0	7.22
1979	6.54	8.26	N/A	5.91
1980	1.64	0.00	N/A	6.26
1981	1.50	5.00	9.0	7.63
1982	3.50	14.73	10.3	8.26
1983	3.76	12.04	12.8	9.10
1984	5.60	17.75	13.2	10.16
1985	6.72	19.40	16.6	11.93
1986	6.82	10.87	15.8	14.19
1987	7.24	21.07	9.6	13.32
1988	7.81	23.42	17.7	12.24

*12 December of year in question.
†Food manufacturing.

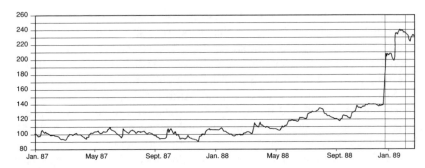

Figure CS1.1 Share performance of Bassett Foods plc before, during and after takeover bid (relative to FT-A All Share Index)

CASE STUDY 2: RICARDO GROUP

Target: Ricardo Group

Sussex-based designer of engines and transmission systems.

Bidder: First Technology

Designer and manufacturer of safety systems and equipment for the auto-motive, fire detection and protection markets.

> **Announcement:** 20 January 1989
> **Value of bid:** £22.7m
> **Defences:** Financial response, legal and/or political
> **Outcome:** BID FAILED

Summary

Ricardo announced interim results and forecast full-year profits and dividends all above expectations. Legal arguments relating to beneficial ownership of shares and concert parties were used to try to block the bid, resulting in a court order freezing 1.9 per cent of its shares.

Background

Ricardo was a firm of consulting engineers with unfunded research repre-senting about 8 per cent of the company's turnover. In June 1988 it reported pre-tax profits of £1.1m, down from £1.4m in the previous year. The com-pany cut its workforce from 545 to 364 and strengthened financial controls.

The business was also being broadened through acquisitions in the UK and US.

First Technology made an abortive bid for another UK automotive design consultancy in 1987. This was followed by the acquisition of an American crash-dummy design manufacturer and an Anglo-Swedish automotive engineering design group. First Technology claimed that major vehicle manufacturers were forming long-term relationships with a limited group of integrated suppliers, capable of handling complete product packages from design to prototype. First Technology intended to combine Ricardo's design expertise with its own experience of production, creating an independent integrated business.

The all-share offer valued Ricardo at about £19m or 131.7p per share. First Technology lifted its stake from 4.9 per cent to 14.9 per cent in a dawn raid and had secured 13 per cent irrevocable undertakings to accept the offer from UEI, CH Industrials and Privatbank. Privatbank sold the 1.9 per cent stake it held for beneficiaries concealed behind a Liechtenstein institution two weeks later. First Technology later increased its share exchange terms to value Ricardo at £22.7m and an underwritten cash alternative of 145.25p per share was attached.

Ricardo argued that its independence from any direct manufacturing involvement was a key to its success. It claimed to work already for all the major players in the industry whereas First Technology had a narrow product range and was dependent on just two major car manufacturers. Ricardo questioned First Technology's judgement in launching a hostile bid for a business dependent on key individual personnel.

Defence

FINANCIAL RESPONSE Ricardo unveiled a sharp recovery in pre-tax profits to £1.11m for the six months to 31 December 1988 compared to the previous year's figure of £262 000. The directors proposed to increase the interim dividend by 35 per cent and said order books stood at a record level of £21m. Ricardo also forecast pre-tax profits of £2.4m, up 118 per cent on the previous year. The total dividend was forecast to increase by 54 per cent.

LEGAL AND/OR POLITICAL The executive of the Takeover Panel had misled First Technology by allowing irrevocable acceptances before the bid announcement. Although new irrevocable acceptances were completed Ricardo used this opportunity to try to persuade UEI and CH Industrials to change their minds. Court orders disenfranchising about 10 per cent of its shares were granted on Ricardo's request under Section 216 of the 1985 Companies Act as a result of unsatisfactory replies received to various Section 212 notices seeking to discover beneficial ownership. The court order covered shares held by CH Industrials and Privatbank. In court CH Industrials argued its replies were the result of an 'honest error' and the court orders were released. A separate court order freezing the 270 000 shares held by Privatbank remained in force. Ricardo also maintained that CH Industrials was a party to an agreement under section 204 of the 1985 Companies Act by virtue of the irrevocable undertakings it gave to First Technology to accept the offer. Section 204 dealt with disclosure obligations arising from an agreement between two or more parties which included provision for the acquisition of shares in a public company by either (or both) of them. The potential implication was that First Technology might have been required to attach a full cash alternative. This argument was not accepted in court and costs were awarded to CH Industrial.

Outcome

At the final close First Technology held shares and acceptances representing 41.01 per cent of Ricardo's share capital and accordingly the offer lapsed. This did not include 1.9 per cent irrevocable acceptances held by Privatbank but did include accidental acceptances of about 6 per cent from a fund managed by Schroders who were Ricardo's advisers. Ricardo later revealed pre-tax profits of £2.56m and merged with SAC International plc in spite of First Technology's attempt to block this move. The defence cost the company £985 000.

Table CS2.1 Financial performance of Ricardo Group, 1978–1988

A/c year ending	Div per share	Net eps (adjusted)	p/e ratio*	p/e ratio (sector)†
1978	0.66	6.86	17.4	7.26
1979	1.69	10.47	17.9	5.60
1980	1.86	10.47	23.2	7.21
1981	2.13	5.65	24.7	11.25
1982	2.34	9.77	25.3	9.84
1983	2.50	8.08	14.9	10.86
1984	2.50	7.05	17.3	9.80
1985	2.75	9.16	13.7	11.24
1986	3.25	12.08	11.8	12.30
1987	3.25	5.97	19.9	12.17
1988	3.25	4.45	26.0	10.40

*20 December of year in question.
†General engineering.

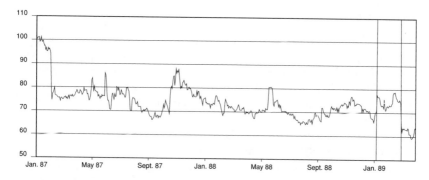

Figure CS2.1 Share performance of Ricardo Group plc before, during and after takeover bid (relative to FT-A All Share Index)

CASE STUDY 3: MARINA DEVELOPMENT GROUP

Target: Marina Development Group

Operator of 11 marinas and owner of 200 acres of land located mainly around the Thames, the south coast, the Hamble estuary and Torquay.

Bidder: Local London Group

Property manager and trader, specializing in business centres.

Announcement: 7 February 1989
Value of bid: £77.7m
Defences: Legal and/or political, white knight, poison pill/shareholding restructure, corporate restructure
Outcome: BID FAILED (bidder withdrew for reasons unrelated to the target's defences)

Summary

With the bidder holding acceptances for 47.7 per cent of the target at the close of the bid announcement day, Marina Development used legal procedures, an exercise of options, and the possibility of a higher offer to prolong the bid battle. The bid was finally blocked when another company launched a bid for the predator.

Background

In the early 1970s, Local London was a member of a concert party which acquired 50.1 per cent of the then issued share capital of Marina Development. New management was installed and £37m was raised through a rights issue. The two Bourne brothers were joint chief executives and founders of Local London. They also each had a seat on the board of Marina Development.

Local London claimed Marina Development was not making sufficient use of land it owned adjacent to marinas, some of which already had planning permission. Local London claimed it had the experience to improve marina operations and take advantage of opportunities for residential and other property developments more rapidly.

In order to avoid dilution and high gearing, Local London's offer was made entirely in cumulative convertible preference shares. Once converted, in July 1991, the issue would account for 35.5 per cent of Local London's enlarged ordinary capital and required the support of its shareholders which was to be sought at an extraordinary general meeting. The preference shares also carried a 'poison pill' element that allowed early conversion in the event of a hostile takeover bid for Local London—a move which threatened to dilute Brent Walker's existing 29.9 per cent in Local London to 22 per cent.

The share exchange valued Marina Development at £77.7m or 521p a share. Marina Development's share price closed at 490p, up 110p on the day. On the day of the announcement Local London lifted its stake from 25.3 per cent to 29.95 per cent and received acceptances from Govett Strategic Investment Trust and Lucas Pension Funds taking its total acceptances to 47.7 per cent by the close. Marina Development believed the offer failed to recognize the full value of its leasehold berth interests and substantial waterfront land bank.

Defence

LEGAL AND/OR POLITICAL The day after the announcement the High Court gave Marina Development an *ex parte* injunction prohibiting Local London from going ahead with its offer and from soliciting any further acceptances. Marina Development claimed the Bourne brothers had used confidential information about a planned revaluation of Marina Development's assets as an opportunity to 'snap up the company at a very cheap price'. Marina Development dropped the court action and was ordered to pay all legal fees when Local London proved that the decision to bid had been taken before the planned asset revaluation. Marina Development called for a full Takeover Panel hearing to discover whether Govett Strategic Investment Trust and Lucas Pension Fund had committed their holding to Local London before the bid was announced. The full Panel dismissed Marina Development's appeal.

WHITE KNIGHT Marina Development claimed it was in talks 'with a third party which might lead to an offer at a higher level'. Although no white knights emerged, the announcement helped to raise Marina Development's share price from 491p to 524p, above the terms of the bid. However, Priest Marians, an acquisitive property company, made a conditional bid for Local London. Priest Marians took its stake in Local London up to 19.33 per cent in a dawn raid and Brent Walker declared an intention to accept the bid in respect of its 29.9 per cent stake. Both the bid and Brent Walker's acceptances were conditional on Local London dropping its bid for Marina Development at Local London's extraordinary general meeting.

POISON PILL/SHAREHOLDING RESTRUCTURE The directors exercised options on 750 000 shares representing about 4.75 per cent of the company's capital, diluting Local London's holding to about 45.5 per cent.

CORPORATE RESTRUCTURE After announcing that talks with third parties had collapsed, some of Marina Development's directors started working on a management buy-out proposal. The announcement caused Marina Development's share price to fall below the offer price, enabling Local London to buy 220 000 shares in the market, taking its total acceptances and shares held to 46.9 per cent.

Outcome

Shareholders at Local London's extraordinary general meeting voted down the resolution to approve the acquisition of Marina Development by two votes to one. In June 1989, Marina Development announced that asset value had almost doubled to 630p per share compared with 318p in the previous year. The results also revealed that the defence cost the company £1.15m.

Table CS3.1 Financial performance of Marina Development Group, 1983–1988

A/c year ending	Div per share	Net eps (adjusted)	p/e ratio*	p/e ratio (sector)†
1983	N/A	N/A	N/A	14.32
1984	N/A	N/A	N/A	15.81
1985	N/A	N/A	N/A	16.48
1986	N/A	N/A	N/A	17.65
1987	0.00	1.80	24.6	17.62
1988	1.00	3.39	57.3	16.91

*7 January of year in question.
†Leisure.

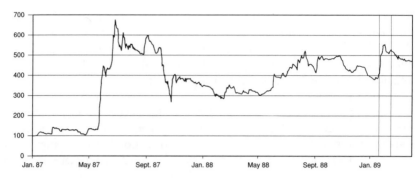

Figure CS3.1 Share performance of Marina Development Group plc before, during and after takeover bid (relative to FT-A All Share Index)

CASE STUDY 4: CHAMBERLAIN PHIPPS

Target: Chamberlain Phipps

Shoe components, adhesives and speciality chemicals.

Bidder: Bowater Industries

Packaging and industrial products.

> **Announcement:** 21 February 1989
> **Value of bid:** £86.6m
> **Defences:** White knight
> **Outcome:** BID FAILED

Summary

Evode, a plastics and chemicals group, made a recommended equity offer for Chamberlain Phipps. The recommendation was withdrawn when Bowater Industries made a higher cash offer. When both offers were increased to similar values, the Chamberlain board reinstated its recommendation of the Evode offer from which it expected better commercial benefits. Evode won its bid.

Background

Evode, a plastics and chemicals group, had a 4 per cent holding in Chamberlain Phipps. Chamberlain had recently announced that its profits were unlikely to change from the previous year's £7.5m because of problems with some overseas operations.

Following some sudden rises in Chamberlain's share price, reasons for which the Stock Exchange was to investigate, Evode made a bid for the company. The Chamberlain share price closed at 197p, having risen 54p from its 143p price two days previously. The following week, on 16 February, the offer was slightly increased, and recommended by the Chamberlain board. Chamberlain shares dropped 7p to 189p. Evode said that the combination of adhesives divisions would create a world player in that market. There were also common interests in footware components and automotive products.

The agreed offer was 10 new ordinary and 21 convertible preference shares in Evode for every 20 ordinary Chamberlain shares. With the price of Evode's ordinary shares down 5p at 186p, and its preference shares at 100p, the bid valued Chamberlain shares at 198p each. Accepting investors would also receive a second interim dividend of 4.1p per share.

Bowater Industries appeared unexpectedly, offering 220p cash per share and gaining a 7 per cent stake in a dawn raid. Chamberlain shares closed 29p higher at 218p. Bowater said that Chamberlain's adhesives business would link with its coating and laminates division, which was largely based in the US. It said it would retain Chamberlain's cash-generating shoe components business.

Increases in Evode's share price had improved the value of its bid to around 214p per share. Nevertheless, Chamberlain withdrew its recommendation of Evode's offer, saying it was unable to recommend either offer. During the bid, Bowater made a £16.4m offer for Viking Packaging. The offer was accepted by the Viking board which controlled over 50 per cent of the shares. Bowater met the consideration from its own cash resources.

On 28 April, both bidders increased their offers. Bowater offered 230p cash per share, declaring its bid final. This valued the target at £86.6m. Evode immediately responded with a 236p offer of 6 ordinary shares, 11 preference shares and the 4.1p dividend for every 10 Chamberlain shares. Chamberlain's share price rose 7p to 228p. Evode also purchased an 11 per cent stake during the day, while its offer was temporarily worth more than Bowater's. This gave Evode a total of 14.9 per cent, the maximum allowed with an equity bid.

Defence

WHITE KNIGHT After the Evode share price had held its value for a few days following the increased bids, the Chamberlain board recommended the Evode offer. On this announcement, Evode shares rose 2p to 191p, while Chamberlain shares remained unchanged at 224p. The Chamberlain directors' combined holding in their company amounted to less than 0.3 per cent.

Chamberlain said that Evode's offer was marginally higher than Bowater's, and offered very attractive commercial benefits.

Outcome

The offers from both bidders closed on 12 May. On this day, Evode could speak for 53.1 per cent of Chamberlain's shares. Bowater could claim just under 30 per cent, of which a substantial proportion was its own holding acquired during the bid.

Table CS4.1 Financial performance of Chamberlain Phipps, 1978–1989

A/c year ending	Div per share	Net eps (adjusted)	p/e ratio*	p/e ratio (sector)†
1978	1.86	6.81	7.8	7.33
1979	2.44	8.32	6.8	8.16
1980	2.69	11.64	5.7	7.05
1981	2.69	4.01	4.6	5.46
1982	2.87	5.98	11.2	27.79
1983	2.87	4.70	8.0	9.52
1984	3.60	11.62	17.6	19.14
1985	3.85	7.78	11.1	11.04
1986	3.85	6.88	10.4	9.74
1987	4.75	9.18	12.0	15.16
1988	5.50	11.53	11.4	12.61
1989	N/A	N/A	9.9	10.28

*21 January of year in question.
†Chemicals.

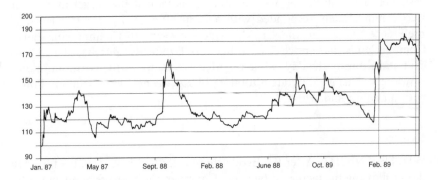

Figure CS4.1 Share performance of Chamberlain Phipps before, during and after takeover bid (relative to FT-A All Share Index)

CASE STUDY 5: LOCAL LONDON GROUP

Target: Local London Group

Owner and manager of 25 business centres, 10 self-access storage centres, portfolios of residential and commercial properties, a 3.5 acre site in west London and a stake of about 30 per cent in Marina Development Group.

Bidder: Priest Marians Holdings

Property development company.

> **Announcement:** 21 March 1989
> **Value of bid:** £110.9m
> **Defences:** None in major defence categories
> **Outcome:** BID SUCCEEDED

Summary

Priest Marians' bid for Local London was prompted by Local London's hostile bid for Marina Development. After losing a resolution to approve the financing of its bid for Marina Development and with Priest Marians holding over 50 per cent acceptances, the board of Local London decided unanimously to accept the offer.

Background

Local London was floated on the Stock Exchange in September 1986 with a market capitalization of about £40m and grew rapidly until the summer of 1987 when its capitalization peaked at £193m. After the stock-market crash in October 1987 the performance of the shares fell behind the average for the property sector by 42 per cent. The company specialized in buying awkward properties and converting them to newly created offices which it let to small businesses. Its short-term source of income was rent charged quarterly in advance at a rate far higher than normal commercial rates and significantly higher than its own longer-term liabilities. Income was also generated from client services including photocopying, message-taking and security and property deals. Local London was in the midst of a hostile bid for Marina Development, in which it held a stake of just under 30 per cent. In October 1988, Brent Walker acquired 29.99 per cent of Local London's share capital.

Priest Marians was a conventional property company. It was interested in Local London's west London site and intended to sell about half of Local

London's other assets including its stake in Marina Development. It needed to borrow funds for the acquisition and had to do so under strict conditions on its gearing, profits and shareholders' funds. Its gearing ratio would have risen to about 110 per cent. Priest Marians offered 550p a share in cash with a loan note alternative, valuing Local London's total share capital at £110.9m. It acquired £3.8m Local London shares in a dawn raid taking its holding to 19.33 per cent. The shares closed at 541p, up 47p on the day. Brent Walker declared an intention to accept this offer but did not give irrevocable undertakings. This would have prevented Priest Marians buying more shares in the market. The offer and Brent Walker's declared intention to accept were conditional on Local London shareholders voting down the bid for Marina Development.

Defence

Priest Marians' bid came just two days before Local London's shareholders were due to vote on the resolution to approve the financing of its bid for Marina Development. Local London rejected the offer, claiming the terms did not reflect the potential value of Local London or the enhanced value of Local London if the bid for Marina Development were to succeed.

Outcome

The resolution to approve the offer for Marina Development was defeated by about two votes to one and accordingly the offer lapsed. On 10 March 1989, the board of Local London decided unanimously to recommend that shareholders accept the offer from Priest Marians, in view of Local London shareholders' rejection of the offer for Marina Development and of Brent Walker's intention to accept the offer from Priest Marians, and because Priest Marians along with its financial advisers owned 20.32 per cent of Local London's share capital. On 4 April 1989, the offer for shares was declared unconditional with 88.6 per cent acceptances and shares held.

Table CS5.1 Financial performance of Local London Group, 1987–1988

A/c year ending	Div per share	Net eps (adjusted)	p/e ratio*	p/e ratio (sector)†
1987	3.00	20.04	68.5	23.93
1988	7.50	31.78	18.6	25.18

*22 February of year in question.
†Property.

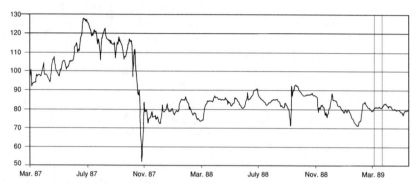

Figure CS5.1 Share performance of Local London Group plc before, during and after takeover bid (relative to FT-A All Share Index)

CASE STUDY 6: BOASE MASSIMI POLLITT

Target: Boase Massimi Pollitt

Advertising and marketing services company.

Bidder: Boulet Dru Dupuy Petit

Privately owned French advertising agency.

> **Announcement:** 29 March 1989
> **Value of bid:** £118m
> **Defences:** Financial response, white knight
> **Outcome:** BID FAILED

Summary

The hostile bid by Boulet Dru Dupuy Petit for Boase Massimi Pollitt followed unsuccessful merger discussions between the two. The target kept its share

price well above the bidder's offers using financial arguments and encouraging
speculation about other potential partners. The US group, Omnicom, even-
tually announced a recommended offer, which the French agency did not
better.

Background

There was widespread realization within the advertising sector that clients
were increasingly inclined to demand greater international coverage in a
wider range of markets. Boase Massimi Pollitt (BMP) had acquired a US
agency, Ammirati and Puris, in 1987, and Davidson Pearce in the UK in
June 1988. It was known to have had merger discussions with Boulet Dru
Dupuy Petit (BDDP), a smaller French agency, over several months.

After unsuccessful discussions, BDDP made a hostile bid for BMP. It
offered 300p cash per BMP share. BMP's share price had risen 18p to
304p over three weeks, after news of a possible offer had emerged. BDDP
had increased its BMP holding to 10.5 per cent. A fifth of BMP's share
capital was thought to be in friendly hands. On the announcement of the
bid, BMP shares increased another 4p to 308p.

During the bid, the smaller private Swiss agency, TBWA, purchased a 2.6
per cent stake in BMP. Wertheim Schroder, the US investment bankers,
purchased a 4.6 per cent stake. These events increased speculation of a
counter bid, and pushed the BMP share price to 320p and above. On 11
May, BDDP raised its offer to 345p and declared this final in the absence of
a competitive bid.

BMP shares rose 12p to 343p. BDDP lifted its BMP holding to 13.27 per
cent, and over the next week to 15.2 per cent.

BMP described BDDP's first offer as derisory and unacceptable. It
claimed both its clients and its employees found the offer unwelcome.
BMP questioned the soundness of the bidder's financing arrangements
which comprised a mixture of new equity, mezzanine finance, revolving
credit and senior debt. BMP contended that a successful takeover would
leave BDDP in breach of covenants concerning interest and cash-flow cover
in its various loan agreements. BMP said BDDP would also have to refi-
nance some of BMP's existing debt. It suggested that if clients were lost, as
seemed likely, BDDP's financial position would be considerably worse.
BMP acknowledged that, since the offer was in cash, its arguments were
of little interest to shareholders. Nevertheless, it met BDDP's banking backers in Paris, who said they were confident that there would be no covenant
breaches. BMP's strategy was seen as an attempt to restrict BDDP's ability
to increase the terms of its offer.

On 19 May, Omnicom, which was the world's fourth-largest advertising
agency group and based in the US, made a recommended bid of 365p cash
per BMP share. Omnicom wanted to strengthen its position in the UK. It

was already well represented in other European countries and in the US. BMP directors were offered attractive positions in a new Omnicom UK subsidiary and on the main Omnicom board. On the day of the announcement, Omnicom acquired a 7.4 per cent stake, directors speaking for 9.53 per cent of BMP gave irrevocable undertakings to accept the offer, and BMP shares rose 23p to 366p. A week later, BDDP extended its offer to 9 June. This was taken as an indication that the French company had not lost interest, and the BMP share price rose 8p to 375p.

Defence

FINANCIAL RESPONSE On 8 May, BMP announced £12.04m pre-tax profits for the year ending March 1989. This was about £0.5m more than analysts' expectations, and compared well with the £6.72m for the previous 15 months. The latter period, BDDP pointed out, included two January-to-March quarters when BMP had, historically, incurred losses. Earnings had increased less than 2 per cent compared with the 12-month period to December 1987. In the same announcement, BMP proposed a final dividend of 7.25p, making a total of 10p against 9p for the previous 15 months. BMP shares remained unchanged at 321p. BMP denounced the 11.9 exit multiple implied by BDDP's offer, and compared it with the multiple of over 20 times historic profits on which another agency takeover bid, by WPP for Ogilvy in the US, was being proposed. BDDP queried the multiple BMP had offered for Davidson Pearce the previous year.

WHITE KNIGHT BMP rejected BDDP's revised offer and stated that it was attempting to remain independent. It had previously indicated, however, that it was in discussions with other potential partners to create a pan-European network. Omnicom was one of a number of potential white knights with whom BMP had had contact for a number of years.

Outcome

On 9 June, BDDP allowed its bid to lapse. Omnicom went on to win control of BMP.

Table CS6.1 Financial performance of Boase Massimi Pollitt, 1983–1989

A/c year ending	Div per share	Net eps (adjusted)	p/e ratio*	p/e ratio (sector)†
1983	N/A	N/A	N/A	N/A
1984	2.66	7.29	33.3	N/A
1985	3.39	10.51	31.5	N/A
1986	2.18	15.58	24.5	N/A
1987	5.75	19.00	17.5	N/A
1988	9.00	16.11	14.8	17.97
1989	10.00	25.24	15.1	14.33

*28 February of year in question.
†Agencies.

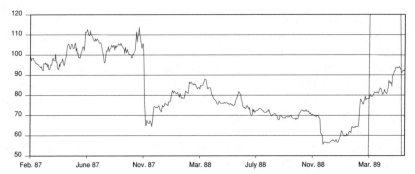

Figure CS6.1 Share performance of Boase Massimi Pollitt before, during and after takeover bid (relative to FT-A All Share Index)

CASE STUDY 7: LAMBERT HOWARTH GROUP

Target: Lambert Howarth Group

Burnley-based manufacturer, importer and wholesaler of footwear, cases and luggage. A supplier to Marks & Spencer.

Bidder: Peter Black Holdings

Yorkshire-based manufacturer and distributor of footwear, homeware, furniture and cosmetics. A supplier to Marks & Spencer.

Announcement: 10 April 1989
Value of bid: £9.3m
Defences: Financial response
Outcome: BID FAILED

Summary

Lambert Howarth issued an asset valuation and followed this up with a profit forecast. Unable to obtain a recommendation from the target's board for a revised offer in excess of the asset valuation, the bidder decided to withdraw.

Background

In March 1989, Lambert Howarth reported losses of £615 000 compared with a profit of £2.1m in the previous year. Sales had increased by 6 per cent but manufacturing margins had fallen sharply due to increased competitiveness of imported footwear and a tighter market in the UK. The company also had problems with overstocking, its suppliers and its luggage operation. Additional costs were incurred on the closure of a factory and the departure of the chief executive. The chief executive and finance director left the company at the end of 1988. Lambert Howarth owned offices in York Way, London, which it was planning to sell.

Peter Black criticized Lambert Howarth's management, pointing to its inconsistent record and inadequate response to changes in the footwear industry. It pointed to its own record of turning around a footwear company it acquired in 1987 and suggested it could do the same for Lambert Howarth. Peter Black claimed the two companies overlapped in many areas and there would be considerable benefits from economies of scale, rationalization of design and pre-production costs, focusing of marketing effort and reduced inventories. If successful, Peter Black would be the UK's third-largest footwear manufacturer. Peter Black was offering one share and 320p in cash for every three Lambert Howarth shares. On the day of the announcement this valued Lambert Howarth at £9.3m or 165p a share compared with its market price of 173p, up 23p. Full acceptance of the offer would involve enlarging Peter Black's issued share capital by 3.6 per cent. Peter Black's bid was preceded by the acquisition of a 5.66 per cent holding in Lambert Howarth by Futura Holdings plc, a footwear and rubber compounds manufacturer. This was later increased to 6.1 per cent. During the bid Mandora Leathercraft acquired a 6.7 per cent stake. Lambert Howarth said the offer was nowhere near a reflection of the value of the company, in particular the value of its freehold and leasehold land and buildings.

Defence

FINANCIAL RESPONSE Lambert Howarth said a revaluation of certain assets yielded a net asset value of £11.7m or 207p per share. The restated asset value included a revaluation of the company's property and reflected Lambert Howarth's decision to account for its 30 per cent holding in a footwear supplier as an investment in an associated company rather than taking it in the books at cost. In its second defence document Lambert Howarth predicted pre-tax profits would be £1.25m for the current year compared with the loss of £424 000 incurred in 1988 (restated to take account of pension costs). A further exceptional profit was expected from the disposal of a freehold property in York Way. The directors forecast a total dividend of 9.5p which represented an increase of 11.8 per cent. It said the company's future strategy would be based on improving manufacturing efficiency, updating designs and selective importation of complementary products.

Outcome

After receiving full acceptances equivalent to 0.63 per cent, Peter Black held discussions with Lambert Howarth's board and its advisers with a view to obtaining a recommendation for an increased offer of 215p per share. In the absence of a recommendation, Peter Black decided to allow its offer to lapse.

Table CS7.1 Financial performance of Lambert Howarth Group, 1979–1988

A/c year ending	Div per share	Net eps (adjusted)	p/e ratio*	p/e ratio (sector)†
1979	2.03	N/A	6.8	8.19
1980	2.35	N/A	3.9	7.60
1981	2.35	N/A	8.9	7.47
1982	2.75	8.41	3.2	10.77
1983	3.33	10.92	10.6	14.74
1984	3.99	15.62	12.5	15.02
1985	4.79	19.88	13.4	15.64
1986	5.75	24.93	11.6	17.28
1987	7.00	23.96	12.7	12.00
1988	8.50	27.36	8.2	9.42

*10 March of year in question.
†Footwear manufacturers.

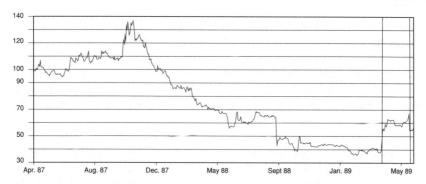

Figure CS7.1 Share performance of Lambert Howarth Group Plc before, during and after takeover bid (relative to FT-A All Share Index)

CASE STUDY 8: PICCADILLY RADIO

Target: Piccadilly Radio

Manchester-based commercial radio company.

Bidder: Miss World Group

Beauty contest, Red Rose Radio (Preston), Radio Aire (Leeds), Red Dragon Radio (Cardiff).

> **Announcement:** 13 April 1990
> **Value of bid:** £39.3m
> **Defences:** None in major defence categories
> **Outcome:** BID SUCCEEDED

Summary

Piccadilly Radio's defence centred on commercial arguments favouring its pending bid for Midland Radio which Miss World Group attempted to block. Miss World Group's bid succeeded with improved terms.

Background

Piccadilly Radio had a two-tier share structure in which only about one-quarter of the total share capital were voting 'A' shares. Also, its Articles of Association limited individual shareholdings to 15 per cent and required holders of voting shares to give first option on their holdings to other voting shareholders. The bid for Piccadilly Radio came at a time of restructuring in the sector ahead of government deregulation and an increase in radio's proportion of advertising revenue. There had been 25 mergers between radio stations over the previous three years and Piccadilly Radio itself had just declared unconditional a £13.1m recommended merger with Midlands Radio Holdings (based in Birmingham and Coventry). Directors had to seek approval of a simple majority of shareholders to increase its share capital.

Miss World Group attempted to block Piccadilly Radio's merger with Midland Radio. Independent Broadcasting Authority rules limited ownership to a maximum of six radio stations or 15 per cent of the total UK market audience, and a combination of the radio interests of Miss World, Piccadilly Radio and Midlands Radio would breach this limit. Miss World Group's initial offer was therefore conditional on Piccadilly Radio's shareholders rejecting the merger with Midlands Radio and secondly on their agreeing to a change in their Articles of Association. The latter condition required a 75 per cent majority.

Miss World Group claimed its merger with Piccadilly Radio would create the UK's second largest independent radio company and give the combined group the kind of critical mass that radio companies required to cope with the deregulation of their industry. It also claimed that another quoted company, Radio City, indicated it would join the enlarged group, creating a radio equivalent of Granada TV in the north-west. Cost savings were anticipated through combined forces in regional sales and marketing.

Miss World Group's first all-share offer valued each voting share at 355p and each non-voting share at 319p. There was a cash alternative of 306p per voting share and 274.5p per non-voting share. Miss World Group already owned 53 per cent of Piccadilly's non-voting shares and had indications of acceptances representing 11.1 per cent of voting shares. Miss World Group later increased its share-exchange terms to 400p per non-voting share. The cash alternative was raised to 344.8p for voting shares and 313.7p for non-voting shares, representing an exit multiple of 54 for the voting shares and 50 for the non-voting shares. This offer was initially conditional on receiving a recommendation from Piccadilly Radio's board, but this and all the other preconditions were removed, enabling the bid timetable to be restarted.

Defence

Piccadilly Radio claimed the offer was opportunistic and would result in fragmented markets and overlapping transmission areas. It claimed that non-regionalized selling had outperformed regional marketing. Piccadilly Radio argued that Miss World Group's proposals would dilute rather than increase its appeal to national advertisers who, Piccadilly Radio claimed, favoured big city markets such as Manchester and Birmingham.

All directors except one decided to recommend the revised offer. The chairman said that the 'increased offer provides shareholders with a valuable opportunity to realize their investments at a price which may not be available in the foreseeable future'. The dissident director acknowledged this but believed that the long-term interests of shareholders, employees and listeners would best be served by the merger with Midland Radio.

Outcome

Miss World managed to defeat Piccadilly Radio's merger with Midland Radio by a majority of just 0.66 per cent. After receiving certain assurances, including a request for the board to stay on, the dissident director agreed to vote in favour of the takeover.

At an extraordinary shareholders' meeting two amendments relating to the company's articles were passed by 89.02 per cent to 10.98 per cent of votes cast. Allied Entertainments was thought to be the only shareholder rejecting the proposal. The bid was declared unconditional with Miss World Group holding acceptances representing 90.8 per cent of Piccadilly Radio's non-voting shares and 74.6 per cent of the voting shares. The bid was declared wholly unconditional after the IBA gave its necessary consent.

Table CS8.1 Financial performance of Piccadilly Radio, 1984–1989

A/c year ending	Div per share	Net eps (adjusted)	p/e ratio*	p/e ratio (sector)†
1984	1.87	2.48	N/A	15.31
1985	2.00	2.80	8.9	15.78
1986	2.00	2.69	11.2	17.38
1987	2.25	4.69	27.1	20.78
1988	3.25	9.08	14.6	16.46
1989	N/A	N/A	35.0	17.34

*13 March of year in question.
†Leisure.

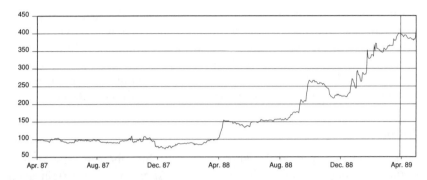

Figure CS8.1 Share performance of Piccadilly Radio before, during and after takeover bid (relative to FT-A All Share Index)

CASE STUDY 9: GATEWAY CORPORATION

Target: Gateway Corporation

Food retailer.

Bidder: Isosceles

Consortium created for bid purposes.

> **Announcement:** 18 April 1989
> **Value of bid:** £2050m
> **Defences:** White knight, financial response, legal and/or political
> **Outcome:** BID SUCCEEDED

Summary

Gateway strongly criticized the proposal by Isosceles to dispose of its super-stores. Isosceles had identified a buyer, which reduced the risk involved in financing its bid. A recommended bid from Newgateway was almost as highly leveraged but not supported with such a practicable method of relieving the debt. Isosceles won an auction which nearly ended in stalemate.

Background

Gateway had defeated a £2 billion bid by Barker & Dobson in December 1987. It was still described as a mixture of widely dissimilar shops. Isosceles, a consortium backed by a number of institutions, made an offer for Gateway with a plan to take part of the group private, dispose of other subsidiaries and the larger superstores, and refloat Isosceles within three to five years.

The offer, worth £1.73 billion, was 195p cash per share, with a partial loan note alternative, and an option to convert the notes into Isosceles shares when the company returned to the stock market. The bid was to be funded by a mixture of equity, mezzanine finance and senior debt. Gateway shares closed 4p higher at 188p. They improved slowly to 195p over the following three weeks. The UK supermarket group, Asda, had agreed to purchase 62 Gateway superstores for £705m, subject to the bid's success and clearance by the Office of Fair Trading (OFT). A transient fall in Asda's share price was seen as indicative of market concern over the price Asda was paying. OFT clearance was granted seven weeks into the bid.

Gateway rejected Isosceles' bid as opportunistic and financially engineered. It suspended and later dismissed four directors of the Gateway Foodmarkets' subsidiary who had expressed support for the Isosceles proposals. It said the bid failed to recognize the group's market position and trading improvement, and undervalued Gateway relative to other takeovers in the UK food retailing sector. It criticized the plan to sell its superstores, claiming that these represented the fastest growth sector of the grocery markets. They were gaining value because of a limited number of available sites, and offered better scope for margin improvement. It suggested the plan would have major adverse tax implications.

On 30 May, Isosceles increased its offer to 210p cash per share and made its first purchases of the target's shares. It also offered an alternative of 195p cash combined with units consisting of ordinary and preference shares in Isosceles. The units were valued by brokers at not less than 15p per Gateway share. The Gateway share price rose a net 7p to 204p. Speculation about a rival bid centred on Europe and the US, as the problem of monopoly excluded the interests of UK food retail groups. The prospects of a management buy-out were impeded by the resulting burden of debt which could then be relieved only using asset sales, the concept that Gateway was currently contesting.

On 19 June, Gateway announced an agreed bid from Newgateway, a vehicle set up by Wasserstein Perella, a US investment bank, and Great Atlantic and Pacific Tea Company, a large US food retailer. The offer was 225p cash per share. Gateway's share price rose 3p to 215p, then to 223p a day later.

On 22 June, both bidders raised their offers. Isosceles raised its offer to 230p cash, or 215p with the equity stub. It declared the offer final and claimed that, having brought its own Gateway stake to 37.6 per cent, it now controlled 44.8 per cent of the target. Newgateway swiftly responded with an increased offer of 235p cash. Gateway shares closed up 11p to 233p. A day later, Newgateway offered 237p per share in order, it was said, to compensate investors for the period between accepting the offer and receiving the consideration. Isosceles commissioned a revaluation of the equity element of its bid. The valuation resulted in an estimate between 30p and 35p, and placed the Isosceles offer at between 245p and 250p per Gateway share. A few days later, Newgateway increased its offer to 242p.

Defence

FINANCIAL RESPONSE Gateway estimated pre-tax profits of £213.7m for the year to April 1989. The figure compared with £185.8m for the previous 53-week period. Analysts had predicted about £200m and the discrepancy appeared to be largely due to a reduced interest charge, which was not fully explained by Gateway. Shares remained unchanged at 195p. The profit estimate was substantiated by the official figure of £214.7m which arrived in the final days of the bid period. Gateway said group trading profits for the first four weeks of its financial year had increased 34 per cent on the previous year's figure and were founded on the improved margins and performance of Gateway Foodmarkets. It promised a 6p final dividend, increasing the total dividend from 8.5p to 9.5p. Gateway announced the results of an independent property appraisal. Isosceles argued that a four-week period was too short for comparisons and pointed out that Gateway's dividend cover was below that of its rivals. It also said that a food retailer was not best valued on its underlying assets. Gateway was later reprimanded by the Takeover Panel, who said the property valuation did not conform to the Takeover Code's requirements for an independent physical inspection.

WHITE KNIGHT The financing for the Newgateway bid was, like that of Isosceles, highly leveraged. The proportion of equity was larger, however, which Gateway stressed was a more solid arrangement. The bid proposal called for a restructuring of Gateway on geographical lines, rather than by store size. Newgateway increased its holding in the target from 10.4 per cent to more than 30 per cent. In passing 25 per cent, Newgateway was in a position to obstruct its rival's ability to take the group private or service its debts, if it were to win its bid.

LEGAL AND/OR POLITICAL When Isosceles announced an increased revaluation of the equity element of its offer, Gateway supported a view that this was in breach of the Takeover Panel's rule forbidding any increase once an offer had been declared final. A formal hearing did not take place.

Outcome

Late decisions by several institutional investors finally gave Isosceles control of 50.9 per cent of the target. Even after the bid was declared unconditional,

Newgateway indicated that it intended to remain an active shareholder and retain its 34 per cent stake.

Table CS9.1 Financial performance of Gateway Corporation, 1978–1989

A/c year ending	Div per share	Net eps (adjusted)	p/e ratio*	p/e ratio (sector)†
1978	1.83	3.53	9.0	9.72
1979	1.90	3.16	17.5	11.94
1980	2.18	4.45	13.2	8.41
1981	2.00	2.61	10.9	12.06
1982	2.40	3.91	20.8	13.73
1983	3.20	4.74	20.9	16.67
1984	3.80	8.13	33.3	19.19
1985	5.80	10.79	25.5	20.36
1986	7.20	14.84	32.6	21.18
1987	8.00	17.36	18.8	23.93
1988	8.50	14.63	14.4	18.02
1989	9.50	16.88	11.4	14.19

*18 March of year in question.
†Food retailing.

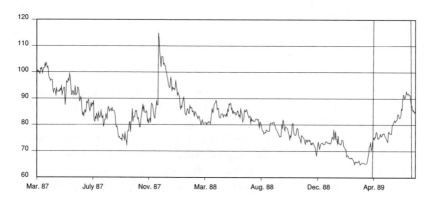

Figure CS9.1 Share performance of Gateway Corporation before, during and after takeover bid (relative to FT-A All Share Index)

CASE STUDY 10: HABIT PRECISION ENGINEERING

Target: Habit Precision Engineering

Manufacturer of specialist engineering products including diamond tools, gem-polishing machines and bed springs.

Bidder: Epicure Holdings

Engineering and construction services based in the UK and Sweden.

Announcement: 21 April 1989
Value of bid: £10.7m
Defences: Financial response
Outcome: BID SUCCEEDED

Summary

Habit's only defence was an operational profit forecast above market expectations. The bidder succeeded by raising its offer.

Background

In March 1989 Habit reported losses before tax of £956 000. Since the appointment of a new chairman in February 1989 the company had disposed of its loss-making computer components business and a day before the bid was launched it announced an intention to sell two other subsidiaries, Doric Unit (bed springs) and Walton Jigs & Tools Ltd. The company was aiming to concentrate on its profitable diamond-tooling business and precision engineering for the aerospace industry.

Epicure's management had turned its loss-making construction services, hotel and property businesses around and then expanded the company through a series of acquisitions. Epicure claimed that Habit's businesses naturally complemented those of Epicure and that Habit's diamond-tooling division had the potential to become a major supplier to Epicure's woodworking tools division. Epicure argued that substantial benefits would be achieved by combining the two businesses, including lower overheads and joint product development. Epicure also believed it could bring an 'experienced management team' to Habit and the combined group could be stronger for being diversified.

The original offer was made on the basis of two new Epicure shares for each ordinary share in Habit, valuing the company at about £9.5m. Habit shares closed at 67p, 1p below the value of the offer. A five-for-two offer was made for the unlisted convertible preference shares, all of which were owned by CIN Industrial Investments. There was a cash alternative of 64p for the ordinary shares and 80p for the preference shares. Epicure already held 11.38 per cent of Habit's ordinary shares.

The offer was later increased to £10.7m by adding a cash element of 15p to the original offer and was declared final. The increased offer was accompanied by a share-buying raid in which Epicure bought a further 14.99 per cent. Habit claimed the offer undervalued the company. Also, it could not understand Epicure's industrial strategy which it said consisted of 'geographically diverse businesses in sectors varying from pistons to property'.

Defence

FINANCIAL RESPONSE Habit forecast that operating pre-tax profits for the year to September 1989 would be a record £1.9m. Total pre-tax profits of £1.25m were forecast. On a prospective exit p/e of 10.8, Habit claimed the offer was an attempt to buy a quality company on the cheap. Epicure criticized Habit's highlighting of operating profits.

Outcome

Failing to find a white knight prepared to make a higher offer, Habit decided to recommend Epicure's increased offer. The board irrevocably agreed to accept the increased offer in respect of its 7.2 per cent holding adding to the 33.5 per cent already committed to the offer. On 6 July, Epicure held 56.08 per cent of the target's shares and declared the bid unconditional. The offer was declared unconditional in all respects on 10 July 1989 with Epicure holding 93.13 per cent of Habit's ordinary share capital.

Table CS10.1 Financial performance of Habit Precision Engineering, 1980–1988

A/c year ending	Div per share	Net eps (adjusted)	p/e ratio*	p/e ratio (sector)†
1980	0.55	1.56	67.2	5.83
1981	0.00	N/A	13.2	8.90
1982	0.25	0.84	N/A	11.58
1983	0.50	2.49	189.3	11.65
1984	1.50	5.01	21.7	12.17
1985	1.75	5.08	14.9	10.79
1986	2.00	7.40	19.3	14.60
1987	2.30	7.08	22.2	15.49
1988	0.80	0.00	12.9	13.07

*21 March of year in question.
†General engineering.

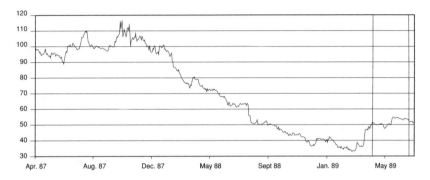

Figure CS10.1 Share performance of Habit Precision Engineering plc before, during and after takeover bid (relative to FT-A All Share Index)

CASE STUDY 11: KETSON

Target: Ketson

Marketing services, public relations and sales training.

Bidder: Moneytab

Consortium of City and Westminster Financial plc (corporate finance), Summer International plc (training and education), Broad Street Group plc (public relations, advertising and marketing).

> **Announcement:** 22 May 1989
> **Value of bid:** £2.8m
> **Defences:** Financial response
> **Outcome:** BID FAILED

Summary

The company having run into financial difficulties, Ketson's shareholders decided to accept a rights issue rather than the terms that were being offered to break up the group.

Background

Ketson's shares were suspended on 25 April 1989 at 19p pending clarification of the company's financial position. Just before the stock-market crash in October 1987 the shares traded at 151p. On 11 May 1989 the company announced that pre-tax profits of £282 000 in the first half of 1988 had been transformed into pre-tax losses of £968 000 in the full year. Shareholders' funds were £5.45m in deficit and debts increased from £1.34m to £5.24m, breaking borrowing limits set in the company's articles. Under intense pressure from banks, Ketson came up with a plan to raise £5m via a three-for-one placing at 10p a share. The shares returned from suspension at 15p, valuing the group at £2.8m.

The loss was mainly attributed to Moorgate Group, a financial marketing and public relations company, acquired by Ketson in August 1988 for £7.4m. Moorgate lost £2.26m before tax in 1988. Moorgate's managing director resigned but its chief executive, who was also Ketson's deputy chairman and largest shareholder with 12.14 per cent, refused to leave and backed the consortium's proposal. Motions to agree the refinancing deal and to remove the deputy chairman were put to shareholders.

The consortium wanted to break up Ketson. Moorgate Group would be sold to Broad Street for £3m plus £2m depending on 1990 and 1991 profits. IETC would be sold to Summer International for £3m plus £1.6m depending on profits. City and Westminster, which owned 29.9 per cent of Summer International, was interested in Ketson's remaining businesses. Its offer was conditional on Ketson's shareholders voting down the board's refinancing proposal.

Ketson shareholders were being offered an equal number of shares in a newly formed vehicle, Moneytab. The three consortium members were to invest £500 000 in return for an initial 10m shares in Moneytab at 5p each but in response to institutional shareholder criticism, the consortium reduced the number of shares it received in line with an ensuing rights issue at 15p a share. If the bid was successful the consortium would seek a listing for Moneytab and make a rights issue on the basis of one share at 15p for every three Ketson shares. This would raise about £1m working capital. Ketson's chairman claimed 'it's the first proposal I've ever seen that aims to reduce shareholder value'.

Defence

FINANCIAL RESPONSE Ketson's chairman informed shareholders that steps had been taken to strengthen the operational management at both group and subsidiary level by improving reporting systems and controlling costs. He was confident that these measures would benefit shareholders significantly. He warned shareholders that if the rights issue were defeated bank facilities would be removed. Ketson pointed out the consortium's offer would involve compulsory dilution and shareholders would be unable to realize their investment as the Stock Exchange would not accept a listing for Moneytab. Ketson also claimed City and Westminster had been associated with three companies which had experienced financial difficulties and Broad

Street had a 'somewhat chequered history'. Ketson believed Moorgate Group and IETC were worth more than the prospective p/e ratio of four that the consortium was offering and the future of Ketson's remaining businesses would be severely limited.

Outcome

Faced with a choice between the present management and unknown management and circumstances, shareholders voted to remove Ketson's deputy director and approve the refinancing package by a majority of 68.8 per cent. The consortium allowed its bid to lapse and Ketson shares fell 1.5p to close at 12p.

Table CS11.1 Financial performance of Ketson, 1979–1988

A/c year ending	Div per share	Net eps (adjusted)	p/e ratio*	p/e ratio (sector)†
1979	0.00	0.00	25.5	N/A
1980	0.00	0.18	14.6	N/A
1981	N/A	N/A	N/A	N/A
1982	0.00	0.00	12.3	N/A
1983	0.00	2.66	N/A	N/A
1984	0.00	0.00	33.5	N/A
1985	0.00	0.29	39.1	N/A
1986	0.00	1.03	212.5	27.07
1987	0.00	3.67	35.4	18.04
1988	1.00	0.00	23.11	5.00

*22 April of year in question.
†Agencies

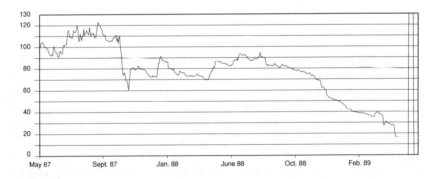

Figure CS11.1 Share performance of Ketson plc before, during and after takeover bid (relative to FT-A All Share Index)

CASE STUDY 12: COALITE GROUP

Target: Coalite Group

Fuel and chemical production, quarrying, waste disposal, vehicle distribution, builders' merchanting and a number of other diverse activities. Also involved in sheep farming and property in the Falkland Islands.

Bidder: Anglo United

Open-cast coal mining and fuel distribution company.

> **Announcement:** 24 May 1989
> **Value of bid:** £478m
> **Defences:** Financial response
> **Outcome:** BID SUCCEEDED

Summary

Anglo United bid for Coalite, which it said had over-diversified to the detriment of core activities. Arguments about the industrial logic and leveraged financing of the deal were later subsumed by a comparison of the respective management abilities of the two sides. Anglo gained sufficient institutional support to win its bid, and promptly proceeded with the disposals it had promised to carry out.

Background

Anglo made its bid saying that Coalite's management and other resources had been diverted away from the company's core businesses to a wide range of unrelated activities. It claimed that this was reflected in Coalite's indifferent record of earnings, which, after inflation, had grown only 2 per cent a year over the last three years. Anglo estimated that the combined group would have 19 per cent of the fuel market, enough to compete more effectively with British Coal who had more than a 50 per cent share.

The offer of 425p cash per share was financed almost entirely by debt. Anglo's market capitalization was only £59m compared with the £427m it was offering for Coalite. The offer was 29 per cent more than Coalite's average price of 330p in January. On the announcement, Anglo increased its holding in Coalite shares from 2.26 per cent to 5 per cent. The Coalite share price rose 15p from 424p to 439p.

On 6 July, having received notice that its bid would not be referred to the Monopolies and Mergers Commission, Anglo raised its offer to 475p a share. This valued the target at £478m. Anglo also added a cash-and-share alternative worth 490p (excluding shareholders' retained entitlement to the 11.25p final dividend). Coalite shares rose 10p to 471p.

The outcome of the bid rested upon ten City institutions, which between them controlled 30 per cent of the capital. A significant number of shares was held by institutions with reputations for being long-term investors, such as Pearl, Britannic Assurance and the Prudential. This last, however, sold half of its holding to Anglo in the final week of the bid, increasing Anglo's holding to 8.4 per cent. Coalite described both offers as unrepresentative of the company's value and potential. It said the bid was not in the interests of shareholders and accused Anglo of asset stripping. Coalite defended its policy of diversification, saying that it had thereby avoided too strong a dependence on the declining fuel industry. It claimed that earnings would have been substantially worse had it not invested in higher growth activities.

Defence

FINANCIAL RESPONSE Two weeks after the bid announcement, Coalite reported pre-tax profits of £48.51m for the year ending March 1989. This was a 6.5 per cent increase on the previous year's £45.53m and exceeded market expectations of around £46m. Earnings had climbed 13 per cent largely due to a fall in the tax rate. A final dividend of 11.25p was proposed, increased from 7.3p the previous year and bringing the total dividend up 43 per cent to 14p. Coalite gave a breakdown of profits showing how income from fuel had declined. It claimed that the increase in its share of the smokeless fuel market indicated that the latter had not been neglected. Coalite shares rose 3p to 441p.

Coalite later forecast a 29 per cent increase in dividends to March 1990, and pointed to properties worth £25m and a pension fund surplus of £64m. The announcement supported Coalite's argument that the offer price was inadequate. It also accompanied Coalite's questioning of Anglo's ability to pay off a bridging loan via disposals, service the remaining debt, and still sustain strong dividend growth. The announcement had only a limited effect in the stock market, where Coalite shares dropped 2p to 462p and Anglo remained unchanged at 52p.

In response to the increased offer, Coalite said that analysts from four leading securities firms had estimated the company's value at between 500p and 600p. It said that the alternative of Anglo shares as a small part of the consideration was not attractive, given Anglo's erratic record of earnings and dividends.

Outcome

Anglo United won its bid following a wave of support from institutional investors. The offer was declared unconditional when Anglo had received acceptances representing 40.26 per cent of the capital, lifting its interest to 51.74 per cent.

Table CS12.1 Financial performance of Coalite Group, 1978–1989

A/c year ending	Div per share	Net eps (adjusted)	p/e ratio*	p/e ratio (sector)†
1978	2.67	13.45	6.4	6.75
1979	2.95	15.53	7.1	7.46
1980	3.70	19.19	8.5	5.44
1981	4.16	19.93	10.1	12.19
1982	4.53	18.16	10.4	8.83
1983	5.05	16.10	9.9	15.21
1984	5.80	21.23	11.7	10.99
1985	6.43	18.70	11.4	9.07
1986	7.50	25.11	12.1	11.53
1987	8.75	28.63	11.8	15.05
1988	9.80	27.16	10.7	10.04
1989	14.00	30.12	14.0	10.76

*24 April of year in question.
†Chemicals.

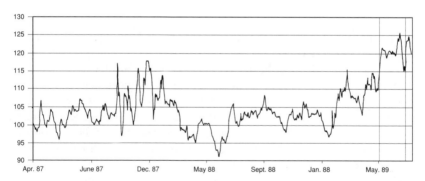

Figure CS12.1 Share performance of Coalite Group before, during and after takeover bid (relative to FT-A All Share Index)

CASE STUDY 13: BUSINESS MORTGAGES TRUST

Target: Business Mortgages Trust

Commercial mortgage company.

Bidder: National Home Loans

Specialist mortgage broker.

Announcement: 5 June 1989
Value of bid: £13.3m
Defences: Financial response, white knight
Outcome: BID FAILED

Summary

National Home Loans made a share-for-share bid for Business Mortgages Trust, for reasons of diversification. Business Mortgages Trust did not announce that the offer was to be contested until it recommended a higher cash bid from the Danish company, Nykredit. National Home Loans sold its 29.9 per cent stake to Nykredit, and the latter won its bid.

Background

National Home Loans (NHL) announced an all-share bid for the relatively small Business Mortgages Trust (BMT), in which it had acquired a 29.9 per cent stake on the previous business day. It said that BMT would enable it to develop a significant presence in the commercial mortgages and banking markets. The terms were two new shares in NHL for every three in BMT. This valued BMT's ordinary shares at £10.3m or about 69p each, representing a 12.6 per cent premium on BMT's pre-bid share price. NHL also made a £3m cash offer for BMT's preference shares. BMT's ordinary share price rose 4p to 65p.

BMT had made a loss of £3.92m in the year to March 1988, largely as a result of a £5.27m provision against bad and doubtful debts. However, for the next six months it had reported a pre-tax profit of £1.25m. Its full-year figures were expected to confirm the company's return to profitability.

On 29 June, the Danish mortgage company, Nykredit, made a 77p per share cash offer for BMT. Nykredit already owned 18 per cent of BMT, having purchased a 15 per cent stake in March. The offer was recommended by the BMT board. Nykredit regarded BMT as complementary to its operations in the UK mortgage market. It promised to protect the employment rights of BMT's staff, and said that consent for its bid had been received from the Bank of England. BMT's shares rose 10p to 75p.

Defence

FINANCIAL RESPONSE BMT's 1989 results, announced shortly after NHL's bid, confirmed the company's return to profitability. BMT said that it expected to resume dividend payments in the current year, following a two-year break.

WHITE KNIGHT Although BMT had appeared to be seeking a cash alternative from NHL, it did not indicate that it would contest NHL's bid until it recommended the rival bid from Nykredit. The fact that NHL gave markedly little criticism of the target was seen as an indication that it was hoping to win a recommendation.

Outcome

On 16 July, NHL sold its entire stake to Nykredit for 83p per share. Under Rule 9 of the City Code, the deal triggered an increased offer at the same price from Nykredit to all BMT shareholders, and assured Nykredit of success.

Table CS13.1 Financial performance of Business Mortgages Trust, 1985–1990

A/c year ending	Div per share	Net eps (adjusted)	p/e ratio*	p/e ratio (sector)†
1985	N/A	N/A	N/A	14.40
1986	N/A	N/A	14.7	16.07
1987	N/A	N/A	15.5	17.95
1988	N/A	N/A	N/A	11.99
1989	N/A	N/A	N/A	12.78
1990	N/A	N/A	N/A	8.80

*5 May of year in question.
†Other financials.

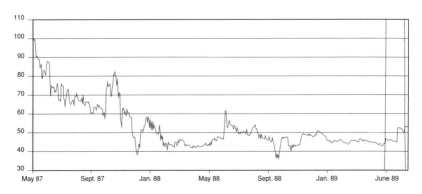

Figure CS13 Share performance of Business Mortgages Trust before, during and after takeover bid (relative to FT-A All Share Index)

CASE STUDY 14: MOLINS

Target: Molins

Manufacturer of machinery for making cigarettes, for packaging and for security printing.

Bidder: IEP Securities

Sir Ron Brierly's holding company.

> **Announcement:** 13 June 1989
> **Value of bid:** £68.8m
> **Defences:** Financial response
> **Outcome:** BID FAILED

Summary

Molins announced good interim results and forecast a doubling of pre-tax profits for the full year. Molins claimed the offer was below net asset value and neglected any income from potential patent revenues in the US.

Background

In March 1989 Molins announced a fall in pre-tax profits from £10.2m to £6m for the year to 31 December 1988, despite sales rising from £103m to £127m. It blamed the fall on a worldwide dip for tobacco machinery. Molins had recently completed a rationalization programme and was concentrating on developing markets in China and Brazil for its cigarette machinery. Its packaging side also continued to make progress. Molins was fighting in US courts for the preservation of rights to patents over flexible manufacturing systems used in computerized production lines. The company said that if successful it could receive substantial income from past and future sales.

In June 1987, Tozer Kemsley Millbourn, a subsidiary of IEP Securities, made an unsuccessful bid for Molins at 300p per share, leaving it with 29.2 per cent. In June 1989, IEP put the stake up for tender at 190p a share with shares in the market trading at 205p. It intended to make an offer for Molins if the stake could not be sold. When no offer was received, IEP Securities made its second bid for Molins. The cash offer was worth 190p a share, valuing the company at £56.3m. The offer was later raised to 230p a share in cash, valuing Molins at £68.8m, and introduced a loan note alternative.

IEP Securities claimed Molins had an 'appalling management record'. It accused Molins of erratic profitability, regular currency losses and significant write-offs on restructuring, resulting in a 23 per cent decline in shareholders' funds over the past five years. IEP intended to keep operating management, replace top management and dispose of loss makers. It also intended to diversify the company's operating base by developing other products outside cigarette machinery. Molins rejected IEP's accusations, claiming the offer did not reflect current and future trading prospects. It said the bid was a 'cynical manœuvre to put the company into play with total disregard for the interests of other shareholders, employees and customers'.

Defence

FINANCIAL RESPONSE Molins forecast pre-tax profits of £13m for the current year. These results included a credit of £2.85m from the application of SSAP 24 concerning pension costs. In its second defence document Molins announced increased interim pre-tax profits of £6.3m compared with £3.3m in the previous year. The board announced an interim dividend of 2.5p and intended to recommend a final dividend of 7.5p per share for the full year. Molins issued a circular showing net asset value stood at £113.6m or 380p a share not including a pension fund surplus and potential income from US patents. The estimated value of surpluses on pension funds was about £55m. Molins also said it had agreed licences to Litton Industries for its flexible manufacturing systems calling for the payment of $11m.

Outcome

The bid failed with IEP Securities holding 34 per cent acceptances and shares of the target. IEP Securities said it was considering several unspecified proposals which had been received for its 33.2 per cent holding. Molins later announced pre-tax profits of £13.9m for the full year.

Table CS14.1 Financial performance of Molins, 1979–1988

A/c year ending	Div per share	Net eps (adjusted)	p/e ratio*	p/e ratio (sector)†
1979	7.90	27.05	7.6	7.99
1980	7.90	22.62	4.3	5.80
1981	7.90	14.77	10.0	9.44
1982	7.90	22.65	12.4	10.89
1983	7.90	15.40	10.1	10.85
1984	7.90	7.19	11.7	10.98
1985	7.90	17.12	14.7	11.71
1986	8.70	17.34	12.1	13.76
1987	9.60	21.99	13.9	15.15
1988	9.60	6.92	11.0	12.36

*13 May of year in question.
†General engineering.

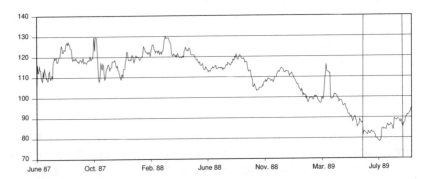

Figure CS14.1 Share performance of Molins plc before, during and after takeover bid (relative to FT-A All Share Index)

CASE STUDY 15: CONSOLIDATED GOLD FIELDS

Target: Consolidated Gold Fields

Diversified UK mining group with interests in gold, stone, minerals, energy and property. World's second-largest gold producer. Owner of 49 per cent in Newmont Mining (US), 46 per cent in Renison (Australia) and 38 per cent in Gold Fields of South Africa.

Bidder: Hanson Trust

Conglomerate.

Announcement: 22 June 1989
Value of bid: £3.5 billion
Defence: Financial response
Outcome: BID SUCCEEDED

Summary

Consolidated Gold Fields pointed to the strong financial performance of ARC, one of its subsidiaries. Hanson succeeded in securing the board's recommendation by raising its offer.

Background

In May 1989, Consolidated Gold Fields (ConsGold) won an eight-month bid battle with Minorco. A New York court injunction prevented Minorco taking control despite having had acceptances for 54.9 per cent of ConsGold shares and clearance from the Monopolies and Mergers Commission, the European Commission and the US Federal Trade Department. Minorco offered £15.50 a share, with £11.25 in cash and the rest made up with Minorco shares. The defence cost ConsGold £30m.

Hanson's strategy was 'careful expansion through acquisition'. In 1986 and 1987 it made three major acquisitions in the UK and US. This was followed by a series of disposals for the next year and a half, eliminating debt and ending up with a net cash position of about £2 billion. Hanson also had approved borrowing powers in excess of £10 billion. Hanson thought it unwise to make pronouncements about its future intentions for companies it was seeking to acquire. Analysts suggested Hanson would keep ConsGold's aggregrate subsidiary, ARC, in the UK and US and sell most other assets. The aggregate business—a mature cash-generative operation with a strong market position—would complement Hanson's other interests in building materials.

Hanson's initial offer was £14.30 a share in cash, valuing ConsGold at £3.1 billion. Minorco gave irrevocable undertakings to accept these terms in respect of the 29.9 per cent it held from the previous bid battle. Minorco also agreed to pay Hanson half of any price above £14 per share if another competitive offer was successful.

Hanson later added a full loan note alternative and warrants to subscribe for 11 new shares in Hanson (at 300p until September 1997) for every 10 ConsGold shares held. On top of this, a special gross dividend of 40p would be paid to shareholders by ConsGold instead of the proposed final net dividend of 27.5p. Each warrant was valued at 60p by the two companies' respective brokers. ConsGold said the revised package was worth £15.30 per share. ConsGold claimed Hanson's first offer completely failed to reflect the value of the company's assets and the bid was a straightforward question of shareholder value.

Defence

FINANCIAL RESPONSE ConsGold focused on ARC to force Hanson to increase its offer. ARC contributed £106m to ConsGold's profits of £300m in 1988 and was expected to contribute £158m in the next year. ARC was earning a return of 18.7 per cent on capital employed and profits had grown on average by 19 per cent a year over the past 10 years. ConsGold claimed ARC's value had risen recently as a result of a government planned expenditure on roads and water. Analysts claimed that ConsGold's other assets were worth at least £2.8 billion, or £2.6 billion based on ConsGold's own estimates in March. This left Hanson with ARC for about £600m on an exit multiple of 4. Analysts' estimates for ARC ranged from £1.5 billion to £2 billion before tax.

ConsGold's shareholders were due to vote on a new form of defence that was devised during Minorco's bid. The defence, nicknamed 'vitamin pill', was a guaranteed earnings scheme. If an earnings per share target of 400p for the period 1990–92 was not met a special net dividend of 6p inclusive of advanced corporation tax credit would be payable to shareholders in 1992. Shareholders would not be asked to vote on the scheme until after the Minorco bid lapsed. The aim of the scheme was to persuade investors that they would not lose out if Minorco's bid should lapse. ConsGold's board decided not to use this defence during Hanson's bid and chose to abstain from voting on the special resolution. At the extraordinary general meeting, 40 per cent of ConsGold's shareholders voted 7:1 against the scheme, but excluding Minorco's vote the vote was roughly evenly split.

Outcome

ConsGold recommended Hanson's revised terms. At the first close Hanson controlled 57.3 per cent of the ordinary shares of ConsGold and declared the bid wholly unconditional. Hanson later took this up to 95 per cent and obtained the outstanding shares through a compulsory acquisition procedure. By 23 November 1989, Gold Fields of South Africa and companies within ARC America had been sold for £1.06 billion.

Table CS15.1 Financial performance of Consolidated Gold Fields, 1978–1988

A/c year ending	Div per share	Net eps (adjusted)	p/e ratio*	p/e ratio (sector)†
1978	8.99	25.38	7.0	6.97
1979	13.21	36.15	11.6	8.58
1980	22.00	57.37	11.3	8.21
1981	24.50	53.37	9.2	8.93
1982	24.50	40.21	7.5	8.14
1983	24.50	29.39	40.8	19.14
1984	24.50	38.18	20.5	12.19
1985	24.50	39.82	17.7	10.60
1986	24.50	35.37	13.4	9.24
1987	27.50	58.49	10.7	20.74
1988	32.00	54.43	15.5	11.30

*22 May of year in question.
†Mining, finance.

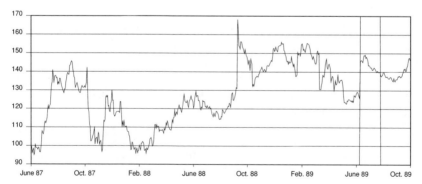

Figure CS15.1 Share performance of Consolidated Gold Fields plc before, during and after takeover bid (relative to FT-A All Share Index)

CASE STUDY 16: RED FUNNEL

Target: Red Funnel

Principal activities were the provision of ferry and towage services, road haulage, warehousing, general engineering and property investment and development.

Bidder: Sally Holdings UK

Owner and operator of Ramsgate port and Sally Line ferry service to Dunkirk. Privately owned subsidiary of Effoa Steamship (Finland) and Nordstjernan Group (Sweden).

> **Announcement:** 23 June 1989
> **Value of bid:** £24.0m
> **Defences:** Financial response, white knight
> **Outcome:** BID FAILED

Summary

Associated British Ports, owner of the harbour where Red Funnel had its mainland ferry terminal, made a higher and recommended counter-bid. Red Funnel also announced its interim results and made a profit and dividend forecast.

Background

Red Funnel (Southampton, Isle of Wight and South of England Royal Mail Steam Packet) had been operating a ferry line between Southampton and the Isle of Wight for 128 years. Of Red Funnel's 735 shareholders, 43 per cent were local residents enjoying free travel on the crossing by holding a minimum of 7200 shares. Another 8 per cent was held by Southern Newspapers located on the Isle of Wight.

Sally's bid for Red Funnel came after the viability of its main cross-Channel service to Dunkirk was threatened by the construction of the Channel Tunnel. It criticized Red Funnel's 'unsuccessful and unwise diversification' into road haulage and engineering and also pointed out that Red Funnel's Southampton–Cowes route was to be challenged by a new rival with a high-speed catamaran and by Sealink which was considering an operation into Cowes from Portsmouth. Sally believed that Red Funnel's share of the market could be increased by better marketing through its 4000 UK travel agencies and investment in new tonnage.

Sally's original terms were 205p in cash for each Red Funnel share, valuing the target at £20.9m. Accepting shareholders could elect to receive their consideration in redeemable loan notes. Sally promised to retain shareholders' fare concessions if its offer was successful. Sally was hoping to maintain a listing by bidding for up to 51 per cent of Red Funnel's equity. Excess shares committed to the offer would be bought by an institutional syndicate led by Tranwood Earl and included Investors in Industry and Globe Investment Trust. Sally had irrevocable acceptances representing 9.28 per cent of Red Funnel's equity owned by Shires Investment. The terms of the final offer were later raised to 236p in cash, valuing the company at £24m. Red Funnel's shareholders were also offered discounts of up to 25 per cent on all Sally's UK products and services.

Red Funnel rejected Sally's terms as wholly inadequate and said Sally was 'likely to be devastated by the opening of the Channel Tunnel and the proposed ending of duty-free sales on cross-Channel services'. It accused Sally of wanting to exchange its poor management, losses, vulnerable route and debts for Red Funnel's management expertise, profits, secure route and cash. The fare concessions were described as 'a worthless gimmick'. It added that a new ferry was being acquired to counter competition.

Defence

FINANCIAL RESPONSE Red Funnel announced interim pre-tax profits of £1.2m, up 14 per cent on the previous year. The interim dividend was raised by 50 per cent and the total dividend was forecast to increase by 25 per cent. Full-year pre-tax profits were forecast to be at least £3.2m, up 12.6 per cent on the previous year, and earnings per share were expected to grow by 20.7 per cent. In its defence document Red Funnel claimed its share price had outperformed the FT-A Actuaries All Share Index by 44 per cent over four years and the offer represented an exit multiple of 14, 'well below the level at which comparable companies trade'.

WHITE KNIGHT Associated British Ports owned 21 UK ports including Southampton harbour where Red Funnel had its mainland ferry terminal. ABP initially signalled its interest by buying a stake of 1.07 per cent in Red Funnel and then made an agreed counter-offer in the form of a share exchange that valued each Red Funnel share at 264p. There was a cash alternative of 260p and shareholders were entitled to retain their fare concessions. Red Funnel's board said it would have preferred to remain independent but the financial terms were such that it had to recommend them to shareholders.

Outcome

During the latter stages of the bid battle Sally entered into negotiations with Sealink to buy its services to the Isle of Wight and with Sea Containers to acquire its Solent business. When, therefore, the white knight emerged Sally decided not to increase or extend its own offer which accordingly lapsed with further acceptances of only 0.52 per cent. On 11 October 1989 ABP declared its offer unconditional in all respects with acceptances of 51.97 per cent of Red Funnel's ordinary share capital. ABP later acquired or contracted to acquire 91.6 per cent of Red Funnel's ordinary share capital with the intention of acquiring compulsorily the outstanding shares.

Table CS16.1 Financial performance of Red Funnel, 1978–1988

A/c year ending	Div per share	Net eps (adjusted)	p/e ratio*	p/e ratio (sector)†
1978	1.49	N/A	9.9	6.69
1979	1.87	N/A	8.1	12.38
1980	2.25	N/A	10.0	8.73
1981	2.50	N/A	10.1	7.50
1982	2.50	4.98	14.1	5.94
1983	3.00	7.57	9.7	16.21
1984	4.00	10.12	8.7	14.79
1985	4.67	9.83	7.8	20.48
1986	5.33	8.05	12.8	14.68
1987	6.67	13.26	10.7	17.30
1988	7.33	13.92	12.1	13.18

*23 May of year in question.
†Transport.

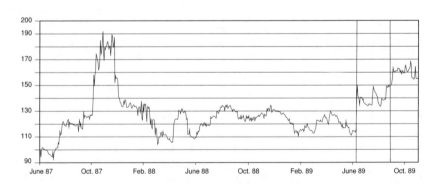

Figure CS16.1 Share performance of Red Funnel before, during and after takeover bid (relative to FT-A All Share Index)

CASE STUDY 17: WARD WHITE GROUP

Target: Ward White Group

Retailer of motor accessories, bicycles, home decoration and DIY.

Bidder: Boots

Retail chemist, pharmaceuticals, health care products and cosmetics.

Announcement: 3 July 1989
Value of bid: £900m
Defences: Financial response, corporate restructure, legal and/or political
Outcome: BID SUCCEEDED

Summary

Following the collapse of discussions to organize a management buy-out, Ward White was left with only its financial forecasts to defend it against a hostile cash bid from Boots. The bidder's recent successful performance was well above average in the troubled retail market, and this record helped it to success.

Background

Ward White's most successful subsidiaries were the Halfords motor accessories store and Payless DIY. The Boots company had an interest in Ward's core businesses for their growth potential and out-of-town sites. It admitted these businesses were generally well run, but said that Boots could provide the cash investment required to develop them. Boots' main criticism of Ward White was that it lacked strategic direction.

On acquiring a 3.5 per cent stake in a dawn raid and bringing its Ward White holding to 10.65 per cent, Boots offered 400p cash per ordinary share, and 137p for each convertible preference share. The bid valued Ward White at £800m. Ward's shares closed up 117p to 442p with speculation about counter-bidders or a management buy-out. Shares in Boots fell 21p to 269p with concern over dilution effects on its earnings.

On 4 August, Boots increased its bid to 445p cash per ordinary share and 152.4p per convertible. This valued the target at £900m. The bidder also provided a share alternative of one Boots share in place of 300p cash. Boots declared that both its new offer and the deadline of 22 August were final in the absence of another bidder. Ward's shares rose 12p to 451p. The Boots share price increased 2p to 301p. Boots took its stake in Ward White to 12.5

per cent. Ward White rejected the revised offer, saying it was continuing to examine other proposals which would improve shareholder value. Analysts noted that a 25 per cent holding in Ward White would allow Boots to block any buy-out proposal.

Defence

FINANCIAL RESPONSE Ward White announced an interim pre-tax profits forecast of £33 m, an increase of 19 per cent over the previous first half, and said it intended to declare an interim dividend of 3.6p, representing a 20 per cent improvement. Ward White shares closed unchanged at 256p. On 13 August, Ward White produced an increased forecast of its interim results. It estimated that pre-tax profits would increase 23.5 per cent to £34.2m, partly as a result of acquisitions. In response to a previous criticism from Boots, the forecast on this occasion included a detailed breakdown of the figures. A final dividend forecast of 10.1p was also given, raising the total to 13.7p compared with 10.5p the previous year. Following the announcements, however, Ward White's share price remained little different from Boots' offer price.

LEGAL AND/OR POLITICAL Ward White appealed against a ruling by the Takeover Panel that Boots, to reach the target for declaring its bid unconditional, could include convertible preference share acceptances. Ward White said this meant that the offer could be declared unconditional even if Boots won acceptances from only 37 per cent of each class of equity. The conversion period for the convertible shares was due to end on 1 September, day 59 of the bid. The appeal resulted in a Panel decision that Boots would not be allowed to count convertible share acceptances until midnight on 1 September, but that it could thereafter, provided conversion notices had been lodged.

CORPORATE RESTRUCTURE For a number of weeks, Ward White was involved in discussions with a number of parties concerning plans for a management buy-out or other reconstruction proposal. On 11 August, however, the company admitted that it was not possible to create leveraged proposals in the current state of the debt markets. There was increasing concern, especially in the retail sector, following the problems associated with other leveraged buy-out deals such as MFI, Magnet and Lowndes Queensway. Upon this news, the Ward White share price fell 10p to 446p, enough to allow Boots to increase its stake by offering 445p cash for immediate settlement.

Outcome

The Ward White share price remained close to the offer price during the last ten days of the bid. Over the period, Boots took the opportunity to increase its holding in the target to 29.9 per cent. With a comfortable level of acceptances for its offer, the bidder was able to declare the offer unconditional.

Table CS17.1 Financial performance of Ward White, 1979–1989

A/c year ending	Div per share	Net eps (adjusted)	p/e ratio*	p/e ratio (sector)†
1979	2.62	21.37	5.3	12.18
1980	4.10	38.32	2.4	8.51
1981	4.10	9.90	9.1	12.45
1982	4.10	7.47	11.2	12.79
1983	4.37	9.53	13.4	16.34
1984	4.93	15.36	12.3	14.69
1985	5.69	17.79	22.2	17.80
1986	6.50	19.47	15.8	20.66
1987	7.50	23.54	17.3	20.85
1988	8.75	28.12	10.8	13.11
1989	10.50	33.25	9.0	11.57

*3 June of year in question.
†Stores.

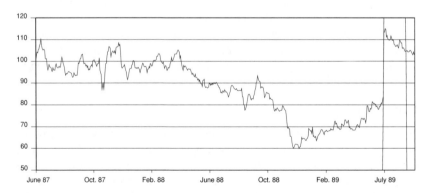

Figure CS17.1 Share performance of Ward White before, during and after takeover bid (relative to FT-A All Share Index)

CASE STUDY 18: BAT INDUSTRIES

Target: BAT Industries

Tobacco, insurance, retailing and paper group.

Bidder: Hoylake

Bermuda-based acquisition vehicle jointly owned by General Oriental Investments, J. Rothschild Holdings, Consolidated Press Holdings, and others. Voting control of Hoylake owned by Anglo Group, a UK quoted leasing and credit company.

Announcement: 11 July 1989
Value of bid: £13 500m
Defences: Corporate restructure, financial response, legal and/or political
Outcome: BID FAILED

Summary

Hoylake made a highly leveraged bid for BAT Industries. The bid was of unprecedented size in the UK, and accompanied Hoylake's general criticism of conglomerates. The bidder was required to win US state approvals for BAT's Californian subsidiary, Farmers Insurance, to change hands. It failed to achieve these, in spite of winning an extension to the conventional UK takeover timetable allowing it to let the bid lapse. A decisive part of BAT's defence strategy was the implementation of a de-merger plan similar to that advocated by Hoylake. In April 1990 Hoylake abandoned ideas of rebidding.

Background

Hoylake's bid for BAT Industries was associated with its general attack on the concept of conglomerates. The object of the bid was to unbundle BAT's original core tobacco business by disposing of the group's other activities. This, Hoylake said, would release the real value of BAT's separate parts to the benefit of shareholders. Hoylake attacked BAT's past expansion strategy. It was particularly critical of BAT's move into retailing. With the exception of Argos, the catalogue retailing business, BAT's interests in this sector had not performed well.

Hoylake's complex offer was worth an estimated 850p a share. For every 100 BAT shares, investors were offered £170-worth of convertible loan stock exchangeable into Anglo shares, £425-worth of senior secured notes taking a first charge on Hoylake's BAT shares, and $418-worth of subordinated notes in Hoylake. The bid would leave BAT shareholders owning 68 per cent of the reconstituted BAT, and 92 per cent of Anglo, which in turn would own 75 per cent of Hoylake. News of the bid caused the FT-SE 100 Index to rise 55.7 to 2250.9. BAT shares rose 206p to 900p. Anglo closed 97p higher at 535p.

BAT said the bid would remove value from BAT's shareholders to the benefit of a mixed group of financiers. It drew attention to a profit 'override' provision giving existing shareholders of Anglo and original backers of Hoylake a preferential share in the returns to Hoylake following the break-up of BAT's businesses. BAT emphasized its earnings record of 18.5 per cent growth in the last seven years. Its total return to shareholders had risen 35 per cent a year. It responded to Hoylake's general attack on conglomerates by calculating five-year total return figures for the top ten UK companies by market capitalization, and claiming that conglomerates had performed best.

Farmers, a US insurance group owned by BAT, was protected by US insurance regulators in nine states. A change of ownership required approvals from the state insurance commissioners. Recent precedents suggested that even if approvals were achieved, the process to obtain them could take many months longer than the 60-day UK timetable for takeovers. A Hoylake plan for an interim trust arrangement, pending the sale of the Farmers subsidiary to new owners, did not receive approval. Hoylake then initiated legal action charging US insurance commissioners with acting unconstitutionally in delaying Hoylake's bid. Hoylake eventually dropped the lawsuits in October, having received rejections from seven state courts.

BAT shares rose 18p to 819p when Hoylake won an unprecedented extension to the conventional UK takeover timetable. The Takeover Panel ruled that the bidder would be allowed to let its existing bid lapse while it sought to clear US regulatory conditions. In the event of gaining such clearances, it could make a new bid within 21 days, and not be bound by the normal rule requiring a 12-month wait before a fresh bid can be made. Hoylake let its bid lapse on 29 September, having claimed control of 2.3 per cent of BAT. Hoylake found a specific buyer for Farmers, Axa Midi Assurances of France, and hoped this would hasten its case. Detailed disclosures were required by the US, however, concerning Axa and companies with large enough stakes in Axa to be able to exert influence.

BAT shares fell 8.2 per cent against the 4.4 per cent market fall on 16 October. Anglo shares fell 84p to 315p. The events underlined doubts about junk bond financing, where a target's equity was being used as security. The following months saw the collapse of the US junk bond market and, in particular, the demise of Drexel Burnham Lambert who featured prominently in the original bid-funding structure.

Defence

FINANCIAL RESPONSE BAT announced interim profits up 20 per cent to £811m, and a half-year dividend payment up 22 per cent to 9.3p. The following month it produced a full-year profit forecast of £2 billion, an increase of 22 per cent on the previous year. Six months later, it was able to substantiate the forecast by announcing 1989 pre-tax profits of £2.04 billion. BAT questioned the value and complexity of the offer, the suitability of the type of consideration for private investors, and the control that existing BAT shareholders would retain over the group following a successful takeover. The Takeover Panel requested Hoylake not to acquire further BAT shares (beyond the 1.25 per cent stake already held) until the Panel ruled otherwise.

LEGAL AND/OR POLITICAL BAT criticized Hoylake's action against US state insurance commissioners, drawing attention to certain filings which had been found to be inaccurate and had delayed Hoylake's progress down the standard approval path. BAT filed a complaint against a law firm acting for Hoylake. The firm had acted for Farmers during BAT's lengthy struggle to acquire Farmers the previous year. The firm gave assurances that its role in the Hoylake bid would exclude issues related to insurance. In the face of projected motor insurance losses, Farmers initiated court proceedings against the California Insurance Commissioner and the imposition of a state-wide motor insurance premium rate freeze. Although BAT acknowledged that there were no direct competition issues involved in the bid, it sought a referral to the Monopolies and Mergers Commission on the grounds that there were wider implications for UK markets as a result of the bid's high degree of leverage. A referral was eventually ruled out, prompting a 14p increase in BAT shares to 827p. BAT encouraged a review of the bid by the US regulatory body, the Securities and Exchange Commission. It pointed out that most of its US shareholders, representing about 5 per cent of total shares, owned their stakes in the form of American Depository Receipts. These were specifically excluded from Hoylake's offer.

CORPORATE RESTRUCTURE On 26 September, BAT announced a plan to slim the business to two activities, financial services and tobacco. Under the scheme, BAT's paper-making activities and the Argos retail business would be de-merged to form two new quoted companies, in which current BAT shareholders would be offered shares. Remaining retailing and other interests were to be sold. The plan included a share buy-back scheme and a further dividend of 20.7p. The latter meant full-year dividends had been increased by 49 per cent. Argos and BAT's paper business were de-merged in April and June 1990 respectively. BAT shareholders received shares in both new companies. The sale of other retailing interests proceeded rapidly. The events effectively deprived Hoylake of a motive for its bid.

Outcome

On 9 April 1990, the California Insurance Commissioner formally refused the permission Hoylake was seeking. On 23 April, Hoylake announced that it would not renew its offer for BAT. Axa confirmed that it would drop its attempt to acquire Farmers.

Table CS18.1 Financial performance of BAT Industries, 1979–1990

A/c year ending	Div per share	Net eps (adjusted)	p/e ratio*	p/e ratio (sector)†
1979	3.84	14.35	5.0	N/A
1980	4.09	13.67	4.3	N/A
1981	4.95	21.48	6.4	N/A
1982	5.92	26.86	5.6	N/A
1983	7.10	32.33	5.5	N/A
1984	8.86	46.08	7.5	N/A
1985	10.41	39.40	6.7	N/A
1986	12.31	44.37	8.5	N/A
1987	14.54	45.02	11.6	14.65
1988	17.30	54.04	8.6	11.04
1989	27.23	68.83	9.8	11.06
1990	N/A	N/A	10.3	12.03

*11 June of year in question.
†Conglomerates.

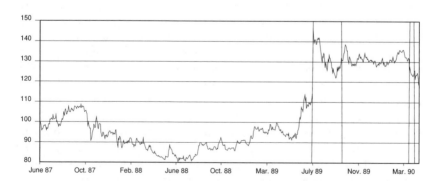

Figure CS18.1 Share performance of BAT Industries before, during and after takeover bid (relative to FT-A All Share Index)

CASE STUDY 19: TILBURY GROUP

Target: Tilbury Group

Construction and building contractor.

Bidder: Lilley

Construction and building contractor.

Announcement: 13 July 1989
Value of bid: £137m
Defences: Financial response, legal and/or political
Outcome: BID FAILED

Summary

Lilley made a hostile equity bid for Tilbury, and two months later increased the offer with a cash alternative. During the bid, Lilley purchased large numbers of Tilbury shares from John Govett. Tilbury vainly questioned the ethics of such purchases, but nevertheless narrowly escaped takeover by making strategic financial announcements.

Background

When Lilley made its equity bid for the Tilbury Construction Group, it made little criticism of Tilbury's management. Tilbury's pre-tax profits had risen 56 per cent to £14.7m in 1988. Over several years it had reported a 33 per cent compound growth in its earnings per share, and it had increased its dividends 37 per cent between 1987 and 1988.

Lilley had announced a £50m pre-tax loss in 1987, and had appointed a new chief executive in Autumn 1988 as part of a management buy-in. Since then it had experienced improved performance. Lilley said that, with Tilbury, the combined group would have a more comprehensive range of services, and much greater financial strength in a market favouring increased company size. It argued that the merger of the two companies was particularly suitable for geographical reasons. Tilbury attempted to devalue Lilley's claim of a geographical match between the two companies by saying that a company simply had to operate where profits were to be found. Tilbury attacked Lilley's five-year record, and described Lilley's present management as largely untried. It also said that Lilley was heavily dependent on US contracts for its profits. Lilley dismissed attacks on its five-year history as irrelevant.

For every 8 Tilbury shares, Lilley offered 33 of its own ordinary shares and 25 convertible preference shares. The latter were valued by analysts at 105p each, making the offer equivalent to 629p per Tilbury share. On the bid announcement, Lilley shares dropped 3p to 70.5p and Tilbury shares jumped 91p from 562p to 653p. This was interpreted as an indication that a better offer or a cash alternative was to be expected from Lilley in the future.

Key institutional shareholders were John Govett, which owned 21 per cent of Tilbury's shares, M & G, which held 12 per cent but was considered to have a policy of backing existing management, and Prolific Asset Management, which owned 6 per cent. During the bid it was disclosed that John Govett had sold a 3.9 per cent stake and Prolific a 1 per cent stake to Lilley close to the announcement date. This, together with Lilley's original 4.9 per cent holding, gave it a 9.8 per cent stake in Tilbury. The Tilbury share price remained well above the value of Lilley's offer, and Lilley was winning the support of few institutions other than John Govett. On 6 September, Lilley increased its offer to equity worth 674p per Tilbury share (then priced at 661p), with a cash alternative of 650p per share and a 10p dividend.

Defence

LEGAL AND/OR POLITICAL Tilbury appealed to the Takeover Panel to investigate whether Lilley and John Govett had acted in concert. It claimed that Lilley had purchased shares at 580p from John Govett close to the bid announcement date. Tilbury suggested that this was part of a plan to avoid attaining a 10 per cent holding or more within a single year. Crossing this threshold would require Lilley to offer a full cash alternative at a price not less than its highest priced purchase in the previous year. Tilbury described John Govett as an 'unsupportive investor', citing also its sale of Tilbury shares to Raine Industries in 1986, only to repurchase shares at a higher price half a year later. Lilley's advisers did not appear worried by the appeal, saying that there had been constant contact with the Panel.

FINANCIAL RESPONSE On 28 July, Tilbury's shares climbed 33p to 678p with the announcement that Tilbury had sold part of its Linwood site in Scotland to Asda, following the granting of planning permission. Lilley's advisers valued the site at £15m. Tilbury questioned the implication that the remaining 335 acres were worth only £4 m, after 15 acres had been sold for £11 m.

On 1 September, Tilbury announced interim pre-tax profits of £10.2m, a 91 per cent increase. It made a forecast for the year of £27m, up 84 per cent. This, in contrast to a previous £22m estimate from analysts, included a contribution from the Linwood site, which Tilbury saw providing a five-year income stream. Tilbury increased its interim dividend to 10p from the previous year's 2.6p. It promised a total dividend increase of 94 per cent to 32p. Lilley argued that Tilbury's profits had resulted from a number of one-off property gains, which could not be sustained because of the declining property sector.

Outcome

Lilley was left 1.2 per cent short of victory when the bid lapsed.

Table CS19.1 Financial performance of the Tilbury Group, 1979–1989

A/c year ending	Div per share	Net eps (adjusted)	p/e ratio*	p/e ratio (sector)†
1979	2.90	N/A	5.4	5.36
1980	2.90	0.00	2.0	4.51
1981	3.24	7.91	N/A	6.87
1982	3.89	10.94	14.0	8.32
1983	4.28	11.99	13.2	10.70
1984	4.66	11.36	10.5	8.35
1985	5.15	13.24	14.0	9.56
1986	6.80	20.98	11.7	17.00
1987	9.20	30.77	17.7	18.48
1988	16.50	41.66	12.0	12.90
1989	32.00	86.76	12.8	9.24

*13 June of year in question.
†Construction and contracting.

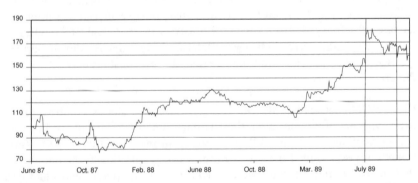

Figure CS19.1 Share performance of Tilbury Group before, during and after takeover bid (relative to FT-A All Share Index)

CASE STUDY 20: A GOLDBERG & SONS

Target: A Goldberg & Sons

Scottish-based retailer, owner of Wrygges (fashion chain), Schuh (shoe retailer), Ted Baker (shirt retailer).

Bidder: Blacks Leisure Group

Sports and leisureware retailer.

> **Announcement:** 31 July 1989
> **Value of bid:** £32m
> **Defences:** Financial response, legal and/or political, white knight
> **Outcome:** BID FAILED

Summary

Goldberg's main financial response focused on the absence of a cash alternative from the bidder but its tactics also included a downgrading of its current trading performance. Goldberg was supported by City analysts and another department store.

Background

Goldberg had developed a successful formula as a specialist retailer but expansion into the south of England coincided with a slump in retail sales. A loss of £2.92m before tax and a reduction in the final dividend was reported for the year-end to March 1989. Blacks' pre-tax profits had also fallen back from £5.35m to £3.97m and debts were about 90 per cent of shareholders' funds.

Blacks intended to use about 40 of Goldberg's outlets in the south to expand its own business. It would improve the combined group's asset base by selling two of Goldberg's freehold sites for about £12m, bringing debt for the merged group down to £2m with net assets of £30m. The book value of the two freehold sites was £6.5m. Blacks also reasoned that its marketing, sourcing and merchandising skills could revitalize Goldberg's operation and cut overheads.

Blacks was making a 22-for-1 all-share offer for Goldberg valuing the company at about £32m or 187p per share. Goldberg's share price closed at 178p on the day of the announcement. The bid would double Blacks' equity. Blacks had secured irrevocable undertakings to accept the offer from Charterhall who held 29.9 per cent of Goldberg's share capital.

Goldberg's main objection was the form of the bid—an all-share offer—rather than the industrial logic.

Defence

FINANCIAL RESPONSE Having previously predicted a return to profitability, Goldberg warned its shareholders that the company was in fact trading at a substantial loss. It warned that analysts' expectations—forecasts ranging from a small profit to a loss of up to £500 000—were over-optimistic. Blacks called on Goldberg to quantify these losses, pointing out that it had the right to withdraw its offer if the trading position of Goldberg had shown 'material adverse change' since its bid was launched. These announcements caused Goldberg's share price to drop 20p to 154p. Goldberg refused to make a forecast but said that between March and August it had incurred trading losses at a rate in excess of those incurred in the second half of the previous year when losses of £3.26m were reported. Black decided to pursue the bid on the basis that Goldberg would have had to quantify the losses if they were sufficiently material. Goldberg then pointed to the 82 per cent 'collapse' in Blacks' share price since July 1987. Goldberg claimed that a stream of acquisitions using equity had diluted Blacks' shares by 59 per cent in just two years. In order to demonstrate that the board's main objection was the form of the offer, N M Rothschild, Goldberg's advisers, wrote to Blacks' advisers inviting them to underwrite Blacks' shares at 6p each, providing a full cash alternative equivalent of 132p per Goldberg share, a discount of 25 per cent to Blacks' offer. It was suggested that Goldberg's board would then consider recommending the bid. Blacks claimed it was unrealistic to expect a cash offer in the light of Goldberg's trading warnings and accused Goldberg of trying to sell its shareholders short by seeking a cash alternative well below the price of Goldberg's shares on the market.

LEGAL AND POLITICAL Charterhall agreed to pay Blacks half the cost of mounting the bid if it failed. Goldberg tried to prove Charterhall and Blacks were acting in concert but the appeal was turned down by the Takeover Panel.

WHITE KNIGHT Fletsland Investments, which owns Lewis's department stores, took a 1.05 per cent stake in Goldberg and announced that an exploratory meeting took place with Goldberg to discuss possible avenues of cooperation. These were rejected on grounds of timing in the context of Blacks' bid. Fletsland considered that there were significant attractions to merging the two businesses and if Blacks' bid were to lapse Fletsland intended to re-open discussions.

Outcome

The bid failed with Blacks receiving valid acceptances in respect of 39.07 per cent of Goldberg's shares. Scottish Amicable said it rejected the offer because of the absence of a cash alternative and the credibility gap between the apparent value of the paper offer and Goldberg's share price which Blacks Leisure was reluctant to underwrite. Several months later receivers were appointed at Goldberg.

Table CS20.1 Financial performance of A Goldberg & Sons plc, 1979–1989

A/c year ending	Div per share	Net eps (adjusted)	p/e ratio*	p/e ratio (sector)†
1979	4.18	13.06	10.3	11.16
1980	5.25	10.15	10.3	9.31
1981	5.25	6.06	13.3	11.76
1982	5.25	5.33	13.5	12.43
1983	5.25	5.76	17.3	16.40
1984	5.25	7.13	11.3	14.02
1985	0.99	1.50	38.8	16.35
1986	4.00	8.24	16.6	20.02
1987	4.75	10.79	18.7	20.33
1988	5.50	11.74	18.3	12.82
1989	3.00	0.00	N/A	11.67

*30 June of year in question.
†Stores.

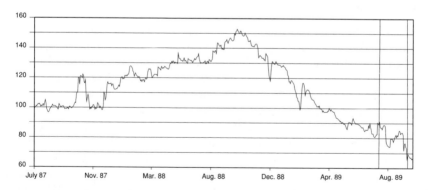

Figure CS20.1 Share performance of A Goldberg & Sons plc before, during and after takeover bid (relative to FT-A All Share Index)

CASE STUDY 21: DE LA RUE

Target: De La Rue

One of the world's largest printers of commercial and security documents and a supplier of bank note machinery, pre-press controls (Crosfield Electronics), fingerprint identity systems (Printrak) and electronic protection.

Bidder: Norton Opax

Specialist printing and packaging.

> **Announcement:** 21 August 1989
> **Value of bid:** £586m
> **Defences:** Legal and/or political
> **Outcome:** BID FAILED

Summary

De La Rue was appealing to the Monopolies and Mergers Commission to have the bid blocked on competition grounds but Bowater Industries rescued De La Rue by launching a rival offer for the bidder.

Background

In June 1989 De La Rue announced pre-tax profits of £26.3m for the year to March 1989, a fall of 59 per cent. The results were accompanied by the resignation of the company's chief executive on grounds of ill-health. This left only one executive director in charge. Norton pointed to the weakness of De La Rue's management and also criticized its diversification strategy. Norton claimed De La Rue's core business (security printing) had been used as a cash cow producing years of flat profits as a result. The cash had been invested in pre-press equipment and fingerprint identification systems, both of which had seen collapsing profits. Just before the bid was announced De La Rue had agreed to sell its pre-press equipment subsidiary, Crosfield Electronics, for £265m. Norton reasoned that the combined business would be complementary both geographically and on a product basis. It intended to proceed with the disposal of Crosfield Electronics and refocus De La Rue on its core businesses.

Bowater Industries held a 25.6 per cent stake in Norton. Analysts suggested that the bid by Norton was a defensive move against Bowater whose stake would be diluted to 13 per cent. This was below the level at which

Bowater could consolidate a share of Norton's profits in its own accounts. The takeover was to be financed by underwritten shares, cash and convertible unsecured loan stock. The value of the offer was about £478m or 335p per share. Following the slump in De La Rue's profits the offer valued the company on an exit multiple of 69. Norton had to call an extraordinary general meeting to approve borrowings for the bid. However, Bowater had been given no warning of Norton's plans to bid for De La Rue and was alarmed at the prospect of Norton borrowing heavily for the bid. To thwart Norton's bid Bowater launched a rival hostile takeover for Norton. The offer was conditional on Norton shareholders rejecting the acquisition of De La Rue at Norton's shareholders' meeting. After Bowater Industries announced its bid for Norton, Norton raised its offer for De La Rue to about £586m or 410p per share in order to 'inform shareholders of the final price' it was prepared to pay for De La Rue. Norton was seeking shareholder approval for borrowings of up to 11 times its adjusted capital and reserves. De La Rue described the first offer as inadequate on financial grounds and unconvincing on the industrial side. The second offer was called 'a desperate gamble by a besieged management'.

Defence

LEGAL AND POLITICAL De La Rue was arguing for a Monopolies and Mergers Commission reference. The acquisition would have given the combined group just under half the UK market for the supply of plastic credit and bank cards. Norton argued that special factors including the possibility of substitution from abroad made this position defensible against charges of monopoly. However, it planned to sell De La Rue's UK cheque printing business, a sector in which it already had a 30 per cent market share.

Outcome

Norton allowed its bid to lapse ahead of the shareholders' meeting when, after counting proxy votes, it became clear Norton did not have a majority of the votes.

Table CS21.1 Financial performance in De La Rue, 1979–1989

A/c year ending	Div per share	Net eps (adjusted)	p/e ratio*	p/e ratio (sector)†
1979	3.70	16.22	12.2	6.11
1980	6.54	19.59	14.0	6.29
1981	6.84	21.57	15.3	11.18
1982	7.19	12.25	15.3	10.43
1983	7.65	15.69	13.7	13.70
1984	8.14	20.82	12.7	14.10
1985	9.77	27.48	12.7	14.47
1986	10.74	27.24	14.6	16.83
1987	12.00	10.87	18.5	27.17
1988	13.25	30.03	16.6	15.57
1989	13.25	2.26	76.3	15.06

*21 July of year in question.
†Publishing and printing.

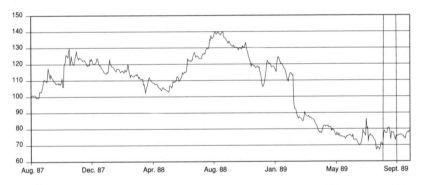

Figure CS21.1 Share performance of De La Rue plc before, during and after takeover bid (relative to FT-A All Share Index)

CASE STUDY 22: NORTON OPAX

Target: Norton Opax

Specialist printing and packaging.

Bidder: Bowater Industries

Packaging and industrial products group.

Announcement: 4 September 1989
Value of bid: £384.6m

Defences: Financial response, legal and/or political
Outcome: BID SUCCEEDED

Summary

Norton Opax, which was involved in a takeover bid for De La Rue, became the subject of a counter-bid from Bowater. It sought a court injunction against one of the bidder's advisers. Norton's bid for De La Rue failed, at which point the Bowater bid was recommended by Norton and succeeded.

Background

Norton Opax had launched a £586m hostile bid for De La Rue and was awaiting approval for the proposed acquisition from a vote at an extraordinary shareholders' meeting. Bowater Industries, the largest shareholder in Norton with a holding of 25.6 per cent, had been given no warning of the bid and was alarmed at the prospect of Norton borrowing heavily to finance the bid. Norton was seeking to gain shareholder approval to take its level of borrowing to 11 times its adjusted capital and reserves. The acquisition would also have diluted Bowater's holding in Norton to below 20 per cent, the level at which Bowater could consolidate a share of Norton's profits in its own accounts.

Bowater claimed Norton was attempting to mask poor margin and cash-flow performance with acquisition accounting and its bid for De La Rue would dilute earnings. By contrast, it said Norton's technical skills would match Bowater's strength in product distribution. Both companies were involved in packaging for the drinks industry and Bowater believed that Norton's personal cheque printing operation would complement Bowater's cheque division. It intended to dispose of Norton's book printing business.

Norton's ordinary and preference shareholders were being offered new convertible cumulative preference shares and cash. The cash and convertible terms were worth 228.75p for each Norton ordinary share and 121.1p for its convertibles. There was also a cash alternative of 225p for the ordinary shares and 119.25p for the convertibles. The offer was conditional on Norton not receiving approval for its proposed acquisition of De La Rue at an extraordinary shareholders' meeting scheduled for the following week. Bowater bought shares in the market taking its holding up to 29.9 per cent, the maximum allowable before a full cash alternative had to be made. The Bowater offer was final unless a rival offer emerged. Norton rejected the bid, claiming the offer did not reflect the value of Norton and urged shareholders to vote in favour of the proposed acquisition of De La Rue.

Defence

FINANCIAL RESPONSE Norton produced an increased and final offer for De La Rue valuing the company at £586m. Norton said 'it was important that we made our shareholders and De La Rue shareholders aware as early as possible that this was the final price'.

Although takeover rules forbid a profits forecast for the enlarged business, Norton managed to get agreement from the Takeover Panel to issue an assumption of De La Rue's profits so that it could be used to counter an argument by Bowater that the De La Rue bid would dilute Norton's earnings.

The figures indicated that the combined group's profits for 1990 would be £76.1m if there were no increase in Norton's performance, giving 12.8p a share earnings. The effect of profit increases of 15 per cent, 20 per cent and 25 per cent were then used to demonstrate how earnings would rise. A 25 per cent increase would lift earnings to 15.6p in 1990 and 19.5p in 1991.

LEGAL AND/OR POLITICAL A year before the bid, Bankers Trust carried out a detailed study of Norton for its management on a proposed buy-out. Norton obtained an injunction against Bowater and its financial advisers, Bankers Trust and Morgan Grenfell, to restrain Bankers Trust from disclosing any confidential information and Bowater and Morgan Grenfell from making any use of this information. The courts overturned Norton's injunction but the Takeover Panel forced Bankers Trust to step down as one of Bowater's advisers. The Panel believed Bankers Trust was in possession of 'material confidential information' about Norton but was satisfied that the information had not passed to Bowater or Morgan Grenfell.

Outcome

Norton received sufficient proxy votes ahead of the extraordinary general meeting to indicate that shareholders would block its bid for De La Rue and consequently allowed its offer to lapse. Norton's board then decided to recommend shareholders to accept Bowater's offer which became unconditional on 28 September with 76.6 per cent acceptances.

Table CS22.1 Financial performance of Norton Opax, 1979–1988

A/c year ending	Div per share	Net eps (adjusted)	p/e ratio*	p/e ratio (sector)†
1979	1.54	N/A	13.2	5.89
1980	2.32	N/A	7.8	6.10
1981	0.52	0.00	12.6	11.07
1982	1.04	0.90	53.8	10.77
1983	1.68	7.44	20.9	14.10
1984	2.33	6.27	17.6	14.63
1985	3.00	8.05	19.1	14.61
1986	3.50	9.90	14.1	16.30
1987	4.00	12.03	15.7	27.85
1988	5.00	11.81	10.8	15.92

*4 August of year in question.
†Publishing and printing.

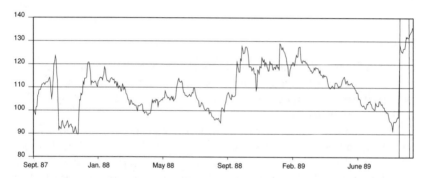

Figure CS22.1 Share performance of Norton Opax plc before, during and after takeover bid (relative to FT-A All Share Index)

CASE STUDY 23: UNITED SCIENTIFIC HOLDINGS

Target: United Scientific Holdings

Manufacturer of armoured vehicles, electro-optical defence equipment and simulation systems.

Bidder: Meggitt

Defence contractor supplying electronics and control systems particularly in the aerospace sector.

Announcement: 11 September 1989
Value of bid: £93.4m
Defences: Financial response, corporate restructure, poison pill, legal and/
or political
Outcome: BID FAILED

Summary

United Scientific's most effective defence was its forecast of large unantici-pated losses. Even though 81.5 per cent acceptances were received the bidder withdrew. The failure of the bid was also attributed to rapid changes in the defence industry during the offer period.

Background

United Scientific had announced interim losses of £5.5m after making provisions for misjudged production hours and delivery schedules on two fixed-price contracts. The company's chief executive resigned when the losses began to emerge.

Meggitt had grown rapidly over the last five years through acquisitions in aerospace and defence. It blamed United Scientific's 'dismal' profits record of the past five years on management. In that period United had three chairmen, three chief executives and two finance directors. With 40 per cent of the combined group's turnover in defence contracts, Meggitt intended to make some disposals.

On the day of the announcement Meggitt's all-share offer was worth 151p per share. A partial cash alternative worth 160p per share and a mix-and-match facility worth 170p per share were also available. United Scientific's shares closed at 176p, up 29p on the day. After the mini-crash in October 1989 United Scientific's shares fell below the value of the partial cash offer but remained above the all-share offer. United Scientific rejected the bid on the grounds of its value and industrial compatibility.

Even though Meggitt's offer subsequently received acceptances from a majority of shareholders, Meggitt decided not to declare the offer uncondi-tional. Meggitt was entitled to do so until acceptances breached the 90 per cent level, at which point the offer becomes unconditional automatically. United Scientific's board initially refused to release further information unless the bidder declared the offer unconditional but when acceptances reached about 81.5 per cent the board agreed to provide limited balance sheet information.

Defence

FINANCIAL RESPONSE United Scientific forecast that losses before tax would not exceed £3.5m after doubling provisions for losses and potential write-offs to £17m on its fixed-price contracts. The results included a profit of £5.5m from a land sale and a credit due to a pension surplus. The extent of the losses alarmed City analysts and Meggitt said it might refuse to proceed until it obtained more information about United Scientific's financial position.

CORPORATE RESTRUCTURE United Scientific had held talks regarding the sale of a US subsidiary (OEC) before the bid was launched. After the bid it announced an agreement to sell the subsidiary for $65m (£42m) to a US competitor. The disposal would enable it to eliminate short-term borrowings and increase its net worth by £9m. Meggitt believed the subsidiary was a valuable part of United Scientific and opposed the disposal. The sale was eventually blocked by the US Federal Trade Commission on competitive grounds.

POISON PILL During the bid the board of US subsidiary OEC revealed it had passed resolutions which allowed directors to receive $2.46m (£1.56m) in golden parachutes if control of United Scientific changed. OEC was sheltered from United Scientific by a voting trust arrangement and proxy board. United Scientific said it had not been consulted about these arrangements in advance.

LEGAL AND/OR POLITICAL United Scientific owned a 65 per cent stake in Avimo Singapore and wrote to the Singapore Securities Industry Council to enquire whether its rules on minority holdings would require an offer to be made for the remaining 35 per cent, on a change of ownership. Meggitt was prepared to buy out the minority, drawing on a £100m credit facility it had arranged before the bid, but the authorities ruled that Meggitt had no obligation to do so.

Outcome

Meggitt decided to pull out of the bid and United Scientific's shares plunged to 80p. The failure of the bid was attributed to the growing gap between Meggitt's partial cash offer and the United Scientific share price following the downturn in the market. Developments in Eastern Europe and Ferranti's problems were also revealed during the bid. United Scientific later announced pre-tax losses of £3.4m.

Table CS23.1   Financial performance of United Scientific Holdings, 1979–1988

A/c year ending	Div per share	Net eps (adjusted)	p/e ratio*	p/e ratio (sector)†
1979	1.72	5.44	17.0	6.68
1980	2.36	7.28	24.8	7.15
1981	2.83	9.97	29.6	10.09
1982	4.00	15.64	39.6	10.14
1983	5.00	17.21	30.1	10.87
1984	5.50	14.32	19.9	10.57
1985	5.70	11.69	13.1	10.46
1986	6.00	0.87	45.1	12.21
1987	6.60	13.82	30.4	15.66
1988	7.30	8.44	15.1	12.47

*11 August of year in question.
†General engineering.

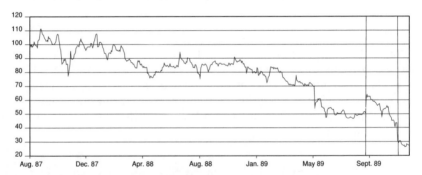

Figure CS23.1 Share performance of United Scientific Holdings plc before, during and after takeover bid (relative to FT-A All Share Index)

CASE STUDY 24: ARMSTRONG EQUIPMENT

Target: Armstrong Equipment

Manufacture and sale of automotive components, industrial fasteners and light engineering products.

Bidder: Caparo Group

Engineering.

Announcement: 14 September 1989
Value of bid: £98.7m
Defences: White knight, poison pill/shareholding restructure
Outcome: BID SUCCEEDED

Summary

Armstrong defended its financial, managerial and strategic record. The lack of a profit forecast, a collapse in the equity market (the offer was in cash) and the rejection of a white knight all contributed to Armstrong Equipment's defeat.

Background

Armstrong had fought off two bids from Wardle Storeys, one in 1987 and a second in 1988/89. Caparo supported Armstrong in the latter £83m bid with its 20 per cent stake, accumulated since 1986. In June 1989 Caparo increased its stake to 29.3 per cent, trying unsuccessfully to gain a seat on the board. Caparo then put its stake up for tender at a price of 185p a share compared with 172p in the market. During the tender offer Armstrong announced its results for the year ending June 1989. Profits before tax were £9.4m, a 65 per cent increase on the previous year's figure of £5.7m. Armstrong had £40m in cash following the sale of its shock absorber division in May 1989.

After Caparo did not receive any offers for its tender sale, it launched a hostile bid for Armstrong at 180p per share in cash. Caparo argued Armstrong's profits were bolstered by the performance of the suspension division. It criticized Armstrong's management, saying 'In the past three years all that the management has achieved is compound growth in sales of 4.8 per cent and a decline in operating margins from 9 per cent to 7.7 per cent. They have no coherent strategy and the pedestrian performance underlying their 1988/89 results is in our view, unacceptable.' Caparo claimed Armstrong did not have the expertise to make acquisitions with its cash and the bid was 'an effective mechanism of returning the cash to shareholders'. Caparo said it did not intend to break up the company.

Armstrong claimed that in the three years since the arrival of new management the group had been transformed. The company's strategy involved the formation of an international engineering group that would manufacture and supply components rather than commodity engineering products which it said were open to threat from low-cost imports. Armstrong also issued a trading statement in which the board proclaimed confidence in the group's prospects for the current year. The final defence document was noted for its lack of a profit forecast. A 13 per cent fall in the stock market in October 1989 depressed Armstrong's share price and Caparo was able to take its stake up to 40.3 per cent by increasing its offer to 185p per share.

Defence

WHITE KNIGHT The day after the bid was announced JH Fenner Holdings, an engineering company, took its stake in Armstrong to 3.75 per cent and later increased it to 6.3 per cent. It offered itself as a white knight with the intention of distributing Armstrong's fasteners through its growing international network. However, Armstrong wanted to remain independent and Fenner was unwilling to launch a hostile bid. Fenner eventually sold its stake to Caparo.

POISON PILL/SHAREHOLDING RESTRUCTURE At the company's annual general meeting the board tried to pass a resolution entitling it to issue 17.7m new shares representing 25 per cent of the enlarged share capital. Armstrong claimed the resolution was similar to those approved at the last two meetings and was not part of the company's takeover defence. The proposal was defeated.

Outcome

Caparo declared its offer unconditional after receiving 77.8 per cent acceptances and shares. Armstrong's board then recommended the offer saying that although the price did not properly reflect either the record of Armstrong or the performance of its management it was not in the interests of shareholders to remain as minority shareholders. Caparo intended to acquire the outstanding shares compulsorily.

Table CS24.1 Financial performance of Armstrong Equipment, 1979–1989

A/c year ending	Div per share	Net eps (adjusted)	p/e ratio*	p/e ratio (sector)†
1979	2.60	16.44	6.7	6.76
1980	2.73	14.44	4.2	7.15
1981	1.50	0.68	7.6	11.43
1982	0.35	0.00	N/A	9.58
1983	0.10	0.00	N/A	10.70
1984	0.60	3.37	20.3	10.63
1985	1.10	7.90	9.4	10.48
1986	2.75	13.36	17.3	12.44
1987	3.30	12.84	21.1	15.75
1988	3.50	10.85	13.9	12.82
1989	5.50	17.11	23.5	12.66

*14 August of year in question.
†General engineering.

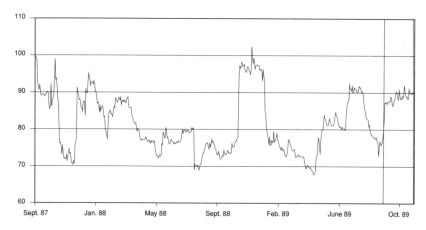

Figure CS24.1 Share performance of Armstrong Equipment plc before, during and after takeover bid (relative to FT-A All Share Index)

CASE STUDY 25: MEAT TRADE SUPPLIERS

Target: Meat Trade Suppliers

Manufacturers and suppliers of sausage casings and butchers' sundries, equipment.

Bidder: Twigrealm

Joint venture set up by Mr Stephen Wingate (property developer) and Mr Freddy Hirsch (butchers' suppliers).

> **Announcement:** 21 September 1989
> **Value of bid:** £9.18m
> **Defences:** White knight
> **Outcome:** BID SUCCEEDED

Summary

Meat Trade Suppliers' board and two financial institutions backed a reverse takeover of the company by Alpha Gamma in preference to the cash offer put forward by Twigrealm. Alpha Gamma's proposals were rejected at an extra-ordinary general meeting and Twigrealm's offer later became unconditional.

Background

Meat Trade Suppliers' core businesses had been in steady decline and the company received a number of offers for the development of its properties. It owned freehold property in Smithfield, a distribution warehouse in Hayes and property in Stafford. The chairman, whose father founded the business, blocked these proposals but in November 1988 he was ousted and replaced by his daughter, Mrs V. Allan.

In March 1989 Meat Trade Suppliers' shares were suspended at the company's request amid speculation that it was negotiating a reverse take-over. The shares were suspended at 430p, valuing the group at £11.3 m. Meat Trade Suppliers had received a proposal from Alpha Gamma, a property developer, but listing particulars sent to shareholders in connection with the proposed deal had to have the signature of all directors. The former chairman who remained as a director refused to sign the proposals. At this stage two long-standing shareholders, Broca Nominees (M&G) and Glyn Mills Nominees (Lombard Street), decided to intervene by requisitioning the board to remove the former chairman as director at an extraordinary general meeting. His resignation was received before the meeting was convened. During the suspension period the company announced the acquisition of a meat trade supplier based in Deptford to provide flexibility over where the company's meat trading operations were to be based.

Twigrealm was formed to bid for Meat Trade Suppliers after shareholders in Meat Trade Suppliers indicated that they would prefer to see an improvement in Alpha Gamma's terms. Twigrealm acquired rights over Meat Trade Suppliers' shares, representing 24.5 per cent of the company's issued share capital, from the ousted chairman. The rights were conditional on Twigrealm launching a successful bid. The bid was conditional on Meat Trade Suppliers' shareholders rejecting Alpha Gamma's proposals. Twigrealm offered 350p in cash for every Meat Trade Suppliers' share, valuing the company at £9.18m. Meat Trade Suppliers' board rejected the bid as unwelcome and derisory. A block of 18 per cent of Meat Trade Suppliers' shares, whose beneficiaries included the former chairman and Mrs V. Allan, were held by independent trustees.

Defences

WHITE KNIGHT Meat Trade Suppliers recommended a reverse takeover offer from Alpha Gamma. The proposed deal involved Meat Trade Suppliers acquiring Alpha Gamma for £12.55m by issuing new shares at 372p. In return shareholders in Meat Trade Suppliers were given an opportunity to partially realize their holdings through a cash offer made on behalf of Alpha Gamma. The revised and final cash offer was made on the basis of 372p per share for two out of every five Meat Trade Suppliers' shares, which valued the whole company at about £9.76m. The deal would have given Alpha Gamma's vendors 65 per cent of Meat Trade Suppliers' enlarged share capital assuming full acceptance of the partial cash offer. Mrs V. Allan, M&G and another trust, representing 35 per cent in total, backed the Alpha Gamma deal. Both bidders claimed they would develop the butcher supply business and property sites. The reverse takeover had to be put to a vote at an extraordinary general meeting.

Outcome

Shareholders representing 61 per cent voted against Alpha Gamma's reverse takeover. This included the 18 per cent held by independent trustees. Meat Trade Suppliers' shares then resumed trading at 365p. The board held discussions with other interested third parties but when no higher offers were forthcoming Twigrealm's offer was recommended. Twigrealm declared the offer unconditional on 24 October after receiving acceptances of 54 per cent.

Table CS25.1 Financial performance of Meat Trade Suppliers, 1979–1988

A/c year ending	Div per share	Net eps (adjusted)	p/e ratio*	p/e ratio (sector)†
1979	7.72	N/A	13.2	10.05
1980	7.88	N/A	7.8	10.28
1981	7.88	N/A	11.5	13.55
1982	6.75	6.90	12.1	14.31
1983	5.25	6.10	15.7	18.21
1984	5.25	6.86	15.5	17.91
1985	5.25	6.85	10.7	23.66
1986	5.30	4.95	16.8	22.80
1987	3.60	3.39	77.9	24.56
1988	3.70	2.55	91.7	15.09

*21 August of year in question.
†Food retailing.

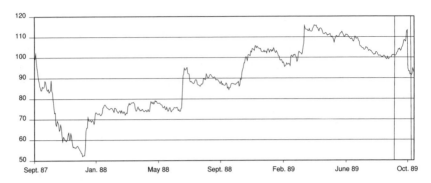

Figure CS25.1 Share performance of Meat Trade Suppliers plc before, during and after takeover bid (relative to FT-A All Share Index)

CASE STUDY 26: DRG

Target: DRG

Stationery, packaging, office supplies and engineering.

Bidder: Pembridge Investments

Investment and acquisition vehicle.

> **Announcement:** 26 September 1989
> **Value of bid:** £697m
> **Defences:** Financial response, legal and/or political
> **Outcome:** BID SUCCEEDED

Summary

Pembridge made a hostile cash bid for the highly diversified stationery and packaging group, DRG. A general slide in share prices left DRG shares below the bid price, and Pembridge was able to purchase enough DRG shares in the market to achieve victory.

Background

Pembridge Investments, a Bermuda-registered vehicle, arranged about £600m of bank facilities which, in addition to its share capital, it used to finance a widely anticipated bid for DRG whose principal activities were in stationery and packaging. The offer was 590p cash per share, worth £697m in total. Pembridge's plans for DRG were to divest it of its peripheral activities and retain a single core business. DRG had recently announced only moderate operating profits, and there were fears that many parts of the company's operations were due to be hit by cyclical downturns. The Office of Fair Trading was called upon to recommend to the DTI whether or not the bid should be referred to the Monopolies and Mergers Commission. There was concern about the highly leveraged nature of the bid, and also the effects on DRG's research and development if the takeover succeeded.

Upon the bid announcement, DRG shares rose 14p to 609p, indicating that the market expected a higher offer from Pembridge or another party. With several companies in the packaging sector looking to expand, there was speculation that a white knight would appear. On 16 October a general slide in the stock market took place, which virtually precluded any possibility of an increased offer for DRG. DRG shares fell from 11p above the Pembridge offer to 21p below it. Pembridge, which already owned 24.6 per cent of DRG's shares, took the opportunity to purchase more at their deflated price. It brought its holding to nearly 30 per cent, beyond which it was not allowed to increase its stake until it had been informed that its offer would not be referred to the Monopolies and Mergers Commission.

On 27 October (the second closing date), Pembridge had won acceptances in respect of 6.3 per cent of DRG shares, giving it control of 36.1 per cent when added to its own holding. Pembridge announced only a short extension of the offer to 3 November. On this date, the DTI gave Pembridge clearance to pursue its bid. The offer was extended once more, and Pembridge continued to buy DRG shares in the market. DRG pointed out that the prospective multiple on Pembridge's offer, given analysts' forecasts of £75m pre-tax profits, would be only about 11. DRG compared this and the historic multiple of 14.9 with the 23 which had been offered recently by Bowater Industries for Norton Opax, a printing and packaging group. DRG took issue with Pembridge's view that DRG had conglomerate characteristics which were not in the best interests of its shareholders. It described itself as a group of well focused businesses which supported a greater degree of technical interchange, investment and financial stability than would the individual divisions operating independently.

Defence

LEGAL AND/OR POLITICAL DRG raised a political issue as to whether overseas companies, based in tax havens, should be allowed to break up British companies with sound records. It hired GJW, a firm of political lobbyists to promote its case among MPs.

FINANCIAL RESPONSE After the slide in share prices, DRG wanted to see its share price recover to a value above the bid price before a non-referral decision from the DTI cleared Pembridge to acquire more DRG shares in the market. The Office of Fair Trading was still deliberating over whether to recommend a referral, and it was thought that DRG was pressing for confidential advance warning of the decision. DRG announced pre-tax profits and a dividend forecast significantly above market speculation. Its profits, it said, would increase 43 per cent to £83m and, following the payment of a second interim dividend of 6p, the year's total dividend would be 27p (up from 12.3p). Pembridge said that the profits forecast was inflated by one-off property profits. The use of property profits, which in the past had significantly helped boost DRG's pre-tax profits, became a central issue during the battle. Pembridge argued that incorporating property profits in an earnings multiple was inappropriate and overstated a company's value. DRG shares rose 22p to 568p, remaining 22p below the Pembridge offer price.

Outcome

When the DTI gave Pembridge clearance to pursue its bid, the DRG share price swiftly rose to match the offer price of 590p. Within days, Pembridge was able formally to announce control of 51.9 per cent of DRG shares.

Table CS26.1 Financial holdings in DRG, 1979–1989

A/c year ending	Div per share	Net eps (adjusted)	p/e ratio*	p/e ratio (sector)†
1979	7.65	N/A	7.6	5.59
1980	8.32	20.33	6.3	4.26
1981	5.87	9.35	10.2	8.68
1982	5.87	7.01	10.8	6.68
1983	5.87	5.84	19.4	10.36
1984	6.3	12.26	12.6	7.99
1985	7.34	21.04	13.6	12.05
1986	8.25	26.65	14.2	19.00
1987	9.35	31.15	17.0	22.20
1988	10.70	35.16	14.1	13.05
1989	12.30	39.80	16.0	13.23

*26 August of year in question.
†Packaging and paper.

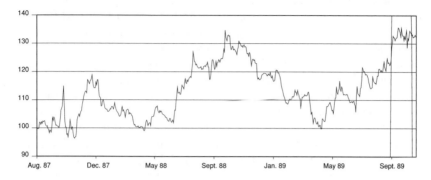

Figure CS26.1 Share performance of DRG before, during and after takeover bid (relative to FT-A All Share Index)

CASE STUDY 27: PEARL ASSURANCE GROUP

Target: Pearl Assurance Group

General and life assurance.

Bidder: Australian Mutual Provident

Mutually-owned Australian insurance company.

> **Announcement:** 2 October 1989
> **Value of bid:** £1240m
> **Defences:** Financial response, legal and/or political
> **Outcome:** BID SUCCEEDED

Summary

Australian Mutual Provident made a cash bid for Pearl which had profound political implications in the UK life insurance sector. In spite of a sound dividend policy record and a favourable actuarial company valuation, Pearl was unable to retain its independence.

Background

The Australian Mutual Provident company (AMP) was looking to expand abroad. It had succeeded in a strongly contested bid for London Life, a mutual life insurance company, earlier in the year. In June, AMP purchased a 13 per cent stake in Pearl, bringing its total holding to 18 per cent. AMP announced a hostile bid for Pearl, offering 605p cash per share. A few days previously, bid speculation had lifted the Pearl price 44p from 508p to 552p. On the announcement, shares gained another 87p to 639p. AMP said it would return Pearl to its leading position in the market, and in particular criticized the fall in Pearl's premiums over recent months.

On 16 October, a general slide in the stock market took place. Pearl shares dropped 28p to 612p, remaining above the offer price, but reducing the margin by which AMP might be expected to increase the offer to win its bid. Pearl controlled about 3 per cent of the UK life assurance market, and AMP about 30 per cent of the Australian life assurance market. On 13 November, the Department of Trade and Industry announced its decision not to refer the bid to the Monopolies and Mergers Commission. There were, however, deeper political implications surrounding the bid, arising from the problem of reciprocity. Whereas any UK insurer was a potential takeover target, most overseas insurers were protected by legislation. On 16 November, AMP increased its offer to 690p cash per share, and launched a market raid which more than doubled its holding in Pearl to 38 per cent. Pearl shares rose 42p to 689p. Britannic Assurance, Pearl's second-biggest shareholder with a 5 per cent holding, said it considered the offer inadequate and would retain its stake.

Pearl rejected the bid, saying that it undervalued the company and its return to shareholders. It said dividend increases had ranged from 19 per cent to 25 per cent in the past four years, and that earnings growth of 35 per cent compound from 1984 to 1988 was the second highest achieved by listed constituent companies in the sector. It attacked AMP's own UK performance with references to a recent survey. Pearl rejected AMP's criticism that premiums had fallen over recent months. It said that AMP was using absurdly selective statistics to support its arguments. Pearl also rejected AMP's claim that it was over-dependent on declining industrial business, indicating that a variety of new products had been successfully introduced throughout the company's activities. Pearl said it was unlikely that it would seek to attain mutual status as part of its defence, as this would reduce accountability and remove an important source of capital.

Defence

FINANCIAL RESPONSE Pearl appointed an independent actuarial consultancy to provide a valuation based on shareholders' funds, future income streams from existing policies, and goodwill. This basis, known as 'appraisal value', had been used in a number of cases to value life assurance companies, but had inherent calculation difficulties associated with inadequate information, the assumptions made, and an element of subjectivity. Permission was granted by the Takeover Panel to include this type of valuation in the target's defence document. The valuation arrived at 765p per share, although shares in Pearl increased only a net 7p to 650p on the news.

AMP pointed out that 311p (or 40 per cent) of the valuation was goodwill, and thus related only to assumed future business. In the same defence document, Pearl announced its intention to recommend a final dividend of 17.5p, lifting the year's total 67 per cent to 25p.

LEGAL AND/OR POLITICAL Pearl won the support of an all-party delegation of MPs who were to speak to the Minister for Consumer Affairs about the bid and its implications for the UK life insurance industry. The MPs argued that the bid was against the interests of policy-holders, because a successful takeover would allow AMP to use Pearl's surplus funds to invest outside Britain. The meeting with the Minister was arranged for 28 November, a week before the offer's closing date. It was on this same day, however, that AMP made decisive purchases of Pearl shares to gain control of its target.

Outcome

Pearl shares remained approximately the same price as the increased offer from AMP. The bidder was able to increase its own holding in Pearl beyond 50 per cent, following purchases from several institutional holders.

Table CS27.1 Financial performance of Pearl Group, 1978–1989

A/c year ending	Div per share	Net eps (adjusted)	p/e ratios
1978	2.81	3.59	
1979	3.40	4.58	
1980	4.00	5.80	
1981	4.60	6.39	Not available
1982	5.50	7.35	for life insurance
1983	6.60	9.10	
1984	7.60	8.05	
1985	8.80	9.65	
1986	10.50	13.08	
1987	12.50	17.33	
1988	15.00	25.66	
1989	7.45	30.48	

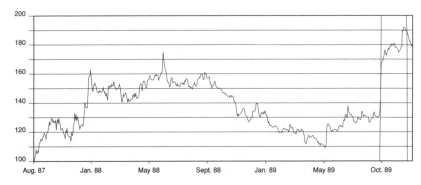

Figure CS27.1 Share performance of Pearl Group before, during and after takeover bid (relative to FT-A All Share Index)

CASE STUDY 28: HESTAIR

Target: Hestair

Owner of various employment agencies in the UK and US. Consumer products division comprising Kiddicraft, Hope, McLaren and Intercraft.

Bidder: Adia Group (Switzerland)

Supplier of temporary and permanent personnel in Western Europe, North America, Australasia and Japan.

> **Announcement:** 20 November 1989
> **Value of bid:** £167m
> **Defences:** White knight, financial response, corporate restructure
> **Outcome:** BID FAILED

Summary

Hestair defended its five-year financial record and continued with its plans of becoming an employment agency. Adia allowed its bid to lapse after BET emerged with a higher recommended offer.

Background

Hestair, a small conglomerate during most of the 1980s, was increasing its focus on employment services. Adia's bid came two weeks after Hestair announced the proposed disposal of Hope and Kiddicraft with the intention of reinvesting the proceeds in personnel services. Adia Group was about to become the world's second-largest staff agency through a merger with another Swiss company. It intended to acquire Hestair using proceeds from the disposal of non-core businesses.

Adia wanted to increase market share in the UK, where it believed there was long-term growth potential. Two-thirds of Hestair's employment agencies were for temporary personnel, the sector of the market where strongest growth was expected. The combined group would have commanded 13 per cent of the total UK personnel market, the same as market leader Blue Arrow. Hestair's US agency would also increase Adia's presence in the US significantly. Adia intended to dispose of Hestair's consumer products division and continue to run the staff agencies separately, gaining synergy through staff training and shared use of facilities.

The offer was made on the basis of 282p per share in cash which valued Hestair at about £167m, a multiple of 10 times earnings. Adia acquired 6.4 per cent of Hestair in a dawn raid. Adia attacked Hestair's recent 'confused' strategy, the fall in earnings per share from 14.5p to 13.3p announced in recent interim results and the 40 per cent underperformance of its share price relative to the FT-A All Share Index during 1989. Hestair believed the offer undervalued growth prospects of the company.

Defence

WHITE KNIGHT On 15 December, BET plc announced a recommended offer for Hestair at 325p per share in cash valuing Hestair at about £192m. A share and loan note alternative was also made available. BET argued that contract staffing was a large part of its service businesses and there was a considerable overlap between the two companies' customers.

FINANCIAL RESPONSE Hestair accused the bidder of 'deliberate use of selective statistics aimed at enticing shareholders into selling themselves short'. Earnings per share had risen 706 per cent since 1985, equivalent to an annual compound rate of 68 per cent. It claimed the share price had outperformed the market over a similar period, making it the eleventh-best performing quoted company capitalized at over £100m. Hestair also announced an intention to increase the number of shares quoted in the US in order to reflect the proportion of its personnel businesses in the US and UK. In the US, employment services traded on a multiple of about 15.

CORPORATE RESTRUCTURE Further to its statement before the bid, Hestair announced the sale of Hestair Hope Limited for £11.65m and Hestair Kiddicraft Limited for £13m. It also planned to sell McLaren in the following year. The company confirmed its intention to become a pure employment agency.

Outcome

Adia held 6.9 per cent acceptances and shares before BET emerged as white knight. After BET launched its recommended offer, Adia decided not to increase its offer and sold its 6.6 per cent holding to BET. BET's offer was declared unconditional on 12 January with BET holding 87 per cent of Hestair's ordinary share capital.

Table CS28.1 Financial performance of Hestair, 1979–1989

A/c year ending	Div per share	Net eps (adjusted)	p/e ratio*	p/e ratio (sector)†
1979	3.38	0.00	N/A	N/A
1980	0.97	2.19	7.7	N/A
1981	0.97	3.46	11.9	N/A
1982	1.93	7.83	9.3	N/A
1983	3.14	9.77	8.9	N/A
1984	3.45	9.35	18.2	N/A
1985	3.45	2.08	22.6	N/A
1986	3.69	11.32	12.6	N/A
1987	4.50	17.91	20.7	24.86
1988	5.40	24.32	13.2	15.54
1989	7.60	28.30	9.7	17.53

*20 October of year in question.
†Agencies.

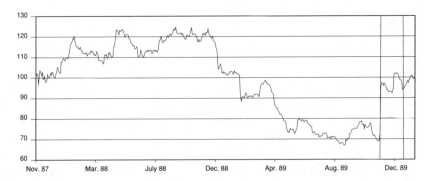

Figure CS28.1 Share performance of Hestair plc before, during and after takeover bid (relative to FT-A All Share Index)

CASE STUDY 29: HIGGS & HILL

Target: Higgs & Hill

Construction, property development, investment and housebuilding in the UK and overseas.

Bidder: Y J Lovell

Construction, property investment and housebuilding.

> **Announcement:** 20 November 1989
> **Value of bid:** £155m
> **Defences:** Financial response
> **Outcome:** BID FAILED

Summary

Higgs & Hill forecast a 67 per cent increase in dividend and issued a valuation of the company exceeding the bidder's final offer.

Background

Higgs & Hill and Y J Lovell were two similarly sized competitors in the construction industry. The bid came four months after merger talks between the two companies were abandoned. Lovell reasoned that the benefit of combining two similarly sized groups with complementary skills was necessary in preparation for increasing international competition. Lovell also believed 'significant' advantages of scale could be gained. The offer was made using underwritten shares, new convertible preference shares and cash, valuing Higgs & Hill at about £138m or 405p per share. The exit multiple was about 10 times 1988 earnings. The offer was later increased to about £155m or 470p a share.

On announcing the bid, Lovell held 2.6 per cent of Higgs & Hill's ordinary share capital. In the offer document the deputy chairman of Higgs & Hill had recommended the offer and gave irrevocable acceptances for his 0.7 per cent holding without informing the rest of the Higgs & Hill board in advance. He was asked to resign, which he did on 4 December. Higgs & Hill called the offer 'opportunistic and inadequate', and informed its shareholders that senior managers of Arlington Securities, Stanhope Properties, Land Securities, Regalian Properties, Hammerson Group, Ranleagh Developments and Capital and Counties had written to Higgs & Hill backing the board against the hostile takeover.

Higgs & Hill also issued a letter to shareholders in both companies from Mr Peter Davis, a shareholder and recently retired director of Lovell Developments. He said that the bid was unwise as it would dilute Lovell's earnings and overstretch its resources. He also claimed that hostile bids were inappropriate in the construction and property development sector because of potential damage to relationships between senior management and clients.

Defence

FINANCIAL RESPONSE Higgs & Hill forecast a 67 per cent increase in dividend, covered 2.7 times. It also issued a valuation based on a profit forecast and an asset revaluation. The construction operations were valued assuming profits of £8.7m, equivalent to 17p per share after tax. On a p/e ratio of 9 (indicative of the sector at that time) this valued the construction side at 153p per share. Its property portfolio in the development and house building divisions was valued at £184m by an independent consultant, a surplus of £51.5m over book value. Four major developments where planning permission had not yet been obtained were valued at an additional £29.5m. The combined after-tax asset valuation was worth 423p per share. Higgs & Hill therefore reasoned the total company was worth at least 576p per share. During the bid Higgs & Hill also announced it had won a new contract worth £70m and had formed a joint property development with Arlington Securities to undertake a venture in France.

Outcome

After Higgs & Hills announced its dividend forecast and valuation, Lovell increased the terms of the offer and bought shares in the market taking its holding to 9.9 per cent (the maximum allowed under the Takeover Code before a full cash offer has to be made). On 22 January the offer lapsed with Lovell holding 34.82 per cent shares and acceptances. City analysts attributed part of the failure of the bid to the lack of a cash alternative, the vagueness about the industrial logic and the striking recovery of construction shares relative to the FT-A All Share Index during the battle.

Table CS29.1 Financial performance of Higgs & Hill, 1979–1988

A/c year ending	Div per share	Net eps (adjusted)	p/e ratio*	p/e ratio (sector)†
1979	1.86	0.00	9.2	4.86
1980	2.31	9.70	N/A	5.48
1981	3.13	14.64	7.5	5.95
1982	4.34	8.51	9.8	9.22
1983	5.30	20.69	9.8	9.11
1984	6.15	21.29	7.7	8.90
1985	6.15	22.78	11.5	11.40
1986	7.50	23.75	11.3	16.85
1987	9.00	31.95	11.6	16.40
1988	12.00	44.98	9.0	11.35

*20 October of year in question.
†Construction and contracting.

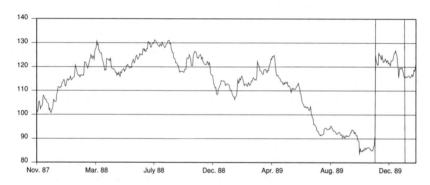

Figure CS29.1 Share performance of Higgs & Hill plc before, during and after takeover bid (relative to FT-A All Share Index)

CASE STUDY 30: METAL CLOSURES GROUP

Target: Metal Closures Group

Manufacturer of metal and plastic bottle tops, plastic packaging, material handling systems and pre-press printing services. Owner of 76.9 per cent of South African listed Metal Closures SA.

Bidder: Wassall

Conglomerate with interests in travel goods and office furniture.

Announcement: 30 November 1989
Value: £45.9m
Defences: Financial response, legal and/or political
Outcome: BID SUCCEEDED

Summary

Metal Closures took the unusual step of forecasting a sharp fall in profits for its current trading year. Much improved prospects were forecast for the following year. Metal Closures also sought to prove the bidder was acting in concert with Suter, from which Wassall bought a 29.9 per cent stake.

Background

Wassall entered into a legally binding agreement with Suter, which held 29.9 per cent of Metal Closures Group, in which Suter gave irrevocable undertakings to accept a cash offer from Wassall at 160p per share.

Wassall believed Metal Closures was a company with good basic products and market share but was 'stifled by top management'. It attacked management's use of cash generated from its South African business on 'misguided acquisitions and fruitless internal investments'. Wassall claimed earnings per share were a quarter of what they should have been to keep up with inflation over the last 15 years. Wassall intended to improve margins in Metal Closures' UK and European operations by reorganization, streamlining and financial controls. This would reduce the group's dependence on its South African operations which generated over half the company's profits but were subject to the falling value of the rand. Wassall would consider disposing of peripheral businesses (pre-press and plastic packaging) if margins could not be improved, though a thorough investigation of all parts was to be undertaken first.

Wassall offered two new ordinary shares in Wassall and 170p in cash for every three Metal Closures' shares. Accepting shareholders were entitled to receive a cash alternative of 160p per Metal Closures' share, valuing the company at a multiple of about 12 times historic earnings. Metal Closures described the offer as opportunistic and derisory. Wassall was accused of trying to reap rewards from £37m spent on capital investments over the last three years.

Defence

FINANCIAL RESPONSE Metal Closures forecast a sharp fall in profits. Profits for 1989 were forecast at £4.5 m, down 45 per cent on 1988's restated profits of £8.2m (previously £7.5m). Earnings per share were forecast to fall by 59 per cent to 6.6p, but dividends were to be maintained at 8.15p. City analysts were expecting profits of £5.7m. These results did not deter the bidder and weakened the target's defence. Metal Closures claimed profits were hit by interest rate rises, higher raw materials costs, an unfavourable exchange rate and difficulties in the materials handling and contract packing subsidiaries. The company denied it was in long-term decline and claimed these results were a temporary aberration. In its final defence document Metal Closures said profits in 1990 would show a 'significant improvement over 1989' due to improved exchange rates and raw materials prices which had become more favourable. It said that it was also on target for price increases on over 80 per cent of its plastic closures output.

LEGAL AND/OR POLITICAL Suter agreed to pay Wassall £150 000 towards expenses of the bid if Wassall withdrew or allowed its bid to lapse. Suter also agreed that if a rival offer was launched at more than 160p in cash Suter would pay Wassall 40 per cent of the difference. Suter gave undertakings not to say or do anything that could prejudice the bid and not to accept any other offer unless Wassall's own bid was withdrawn or lapsed. Metal Closures sought to prove Suter and Wassall were acting in concert but this claim was rejected by the Takeover Panel.

Outcome

With Metal Closures' share price below the cash and share offer but above the cash alternative, Wassall bought 9.96 per cent of Metal Closures' equity in the market (the maximum allowable without making a cash offer for the outstanding shares at the same level). The offer was declared final and an early closing date was announced. On 24 January, Wassall declared the offer unconditional after gaining late acceptances from shareholders representing a total of 51.09 per cent of Metal Closures' equity. Following discussions between the two boards, directors of Metal Closures decided to recommend that its shareholders accept the offer.

Table CS30.1 Financial performance of Metal Closures, 1979–1988

A/c year ending	Div per share	Net eps (adjusted)	p/e ratio*	p/e ratio (sector)†
1979	4.50	16.97	8.2	5.24
1980	4.50	13.95	7.0	4.45
1981	4.75	15.26	8.2	7.70
1982	4.75	13.14	10.2	6.45
1983	5.25	13.30	9.7	11.27
1984	5.58	13.92	9.5	8.05
1985	5.58	6.90	8.1	12.41
1986	6.17	9.12	13.2	18.29
1987	7.40	11.82	13.8	15.95
1988	8.15	14.88	15.6	12.80

*30 October of year in question.
†Packaging and paper.

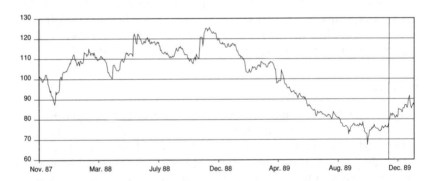

Figure CS30.1 Share performance of Metal Closures Group plc before, during and after takeover bid (relative to FT-A All Share Index)

CASE STUDY 31: DIXONS

Target: Dixons

Retailer of electrical equipment and related goods.

Bidder: Kingfisher

Retailer of household, do-it-yourself, electrical and pharmaceutical goods.

Announcement: 6 December 1989
Value of bid: £568m
Defences: Financial response, legal and/or political
Outcome: BID FAILED

Summary

Kingfisher made a cash offer for Dixons, which resisted the bid with vigorous criticisms of Kingfisher's record. As the target was already the market-share leader in UK consumer electronics, the bid was referred to the Monopolies and Mergers Commission (MMC) and eventually blocked.

Background

Kingfisher and Dixons were both major retailers of electronic equipment. Kingfisher owned Woolworths, B & Q, Superdrug, Comet and Laskys. Dixons had acquired Currys, and was the market-share leader in UK consumer electronics. It also owned the Silo chain which gave it a significant presence in the US.

After Dixons had bid for Woolworths (the former name of Kingfisher) in 1986, the two companies had seen somewhat different fortunes. Dixons appeared to have suffered more from the downturn in the market caused by high interest rates, a surplus of capacity, and a lack of new products. The Dixons share price had fallen from 320p to 120p in the three years. Kingfisher argued that Dixons' poor performance was not entirely due to market trends and that the company had an even bleaker future under current management.

Prior to its bid, Kingfisher held no shares in Dixons. Kingfisher offered 120p for each of Dixons' ordinary shares, valuing the latter at £460m. It also offered 115 new 8.75p preference shares for every 200 Dixons 5p preference shares. Throughout the battle the Dixons' share price held at between 135p and 140p, indicating that the City expected Kingfisher to raise its offer to a similar level to clinch the deal. At such a level, however, Kingfisher would have seen its earnings per share diminish by up to 15 per cent.

Dixons accused Kingfisher of opportunism in using a temporary cyclical downturn in consumer electronics, and unfairly analysing Dixons over a short and recent time period. It alleged that Kingfisher had used a misleading method in its comparison of Dixons' incomes, having compared financial services income before overheads against retail segment income after overheads. Dixons claimed that it remained a good investment, and was well placed to take advantage of the expected market upturn in the 1990s, caused by new technology and demand for electrical gadgets.

In a second defence document, Dixons attacked the performance records of Woolworths and Comet. It claimed that Woolworths had failed in all three of its strategic objectives set in 1986, that Comet's sales per square foot had been in continual decline, that Comet had grown only by cumbersome acquisitions, and that Comet's own brand name, Proline, had failed to become established. The document also challenged Kingfisher to disclose separately its own income from credit commissions and extended warranties after its criticism of Dixons along those lines.

Defence

FINANCIAL RESPONSE On 8 January, Dixons announced a profits forecast of not less than £70m. This, said Dixons, differed from the £40m estimated by analysts because of reduced claims on extended warranty policies. The total dividend was promised to increase by 18 per cent to 5.6p. Dixons' interim results were announced the next day, with turnover up slightly and profits down 24 per cent to £32 m. The City's response was moderately favourable, and the share price rose slightly.

LEGAL AND/OR POLITICAL During the bid, both Dixons and King-fisher were keen to promote their case with the Secretary of State for Trade and Industry, Mr Ridley, who was deliberating over whether or not to initiate an MMC investigation. The arguments centred on certain key issues: whether, as a result of acquisition, Kingfisher would have more than 25 per cent of the UK consumer electronics market; its high market share of certain product groups; its 70–80 per cent of out-of-town sites; and the possibility of greater buying power, the benefits of which might not be passed on to the consumer. Newspapers speculated that Kingfisher would never have made the bid without first receiving informal clearance from the Office of Fair Trading. Dixons stressed that it was to have pre-sold Comet to avoid referral of its reverse bid in 1986. Dixons was asked to clarify that this arrangement was based on its own assumptions, and not on instructions from the OFT.

Outcome

The MMC was eventually asked to investigate on 16 January when the bid lapsed, and to report by the end of April. It was not until 24 May 1990 that Mr Ridley blocked the bid, and enforced on Kingfisher a maximum allow-able holding of 15 per cent in Dixons.

Table CS31.1 Financial performance of Dixons, 1979–1989

A/c year ending	Div per share	Net eps (adjusted)	p/e ratio*	p/e ratio (sector)†
1979	0.68	4.63	7.8	8.99
1980	0.79	4.56	11.2	10.56
1981	0.83	3.99	12.3	10.81
1982	0.90	4.80	21.5	17.09
1983	0.97	5.66	15.7	16.43
1984	1.22	7.25	18.6	15.69
1985	1.46	8.69	31.8	20.55
1986	2.92	13.70	27.6	19.22
1987	3.97	19.21	13.5	14.99
1988	4.30	16.08	9.1	11.57
1989	4.73	11.65	10.1	11.76

*6 November of year in question.
†Stores.

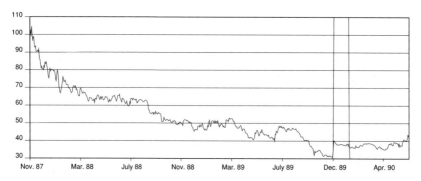

Figure CS31.1 Share performance of Dixons Group before, during and after takeover bid (relative to FT-A All Share Index)

CASE STUDY 32: COLONNADE DEVELOPMENT CAPITAL

Target: Colonnade Development Capital

Investment company.

Bidder: Stratagem Group

Investment company.

Announcement: 22 December 1989
Value of bid: £8.24m
Defences: Corporate restructure, financial response, legal and/or political
Outcome: BID SUCCEEDED

Summary

Colonnade was underperforming, but announced a reorganization plan to which many of its institutional shareholders objected. The objectors favoured Colonnade's liquidation, and one of them, the Stratagem Investment Group, made a mixed bid to effect this. Although Colonnade withdrew the plan and offered alternative arrangements, Stratagem continued its challenge with an increased offer, and won control.

Background

Colonnade was a small quoted investment company, a subsidiary of British and Commonwealth Holdings (B & C), and managed by B & C Development Capital. Most of its shareholders were institutional, and its chairman was also second-in-command at B & C. Colonnade announced that its share price of 120p reflected only 62 per cent of its net assets, and because of this it intended to reorganize by bringing B & C's managers and assets into Colonnade. B & C's own shares were down at 98p from a 242p high for 1989. The management team of B & C Development Capital was to join Colonnade full-time, acquiring B & C's 8.7 per cent stake at 120p a share with performance-related options for further shares.

Stratagem, which owned 4.5 per cent of Colonnade, said the plan was not in the interests of the Colonnade shareholders, only of B & C. Legal and General, holding 4.7 per cent of Colonnade, also queried the plan. It felt that more time should be given to consider the arrangements, and that there should be more evidence of independent advice. Other objectors to the plan included Merseyside Superannuation Fund (owning 9.9 per cent), and South Yorkshire Pensions Authority (with 7.3 per cent). All objectors felt that liquidation of Colonnade was preferable, as cash accounted for nearly £4m of Colonnade's £9.75m net asset value.

Stratagem's first offer for each Colonnade share was 42p cash and 100p nominal of convertible loan notes. The latter component and the interest on it would provide a mechanism for distributing the net surplus upon liquidation. Later, on 26 January, Stratagem made a straight cash bid of 163p per share.

Defence

CORPORATE RESTRUCTURE Colonnade denied that its reorganization plan was only in the interests of B & C, saying that the reorganized group would be worth £9.75m in net assets, or 193p per share. It said that liquidation might not realize the full value of some of its unquoted investments. When it appeared that the required 50 per cent shareholders' approval would not be forthcoming, Colonnade withdrew its reorganization plan, stressing that alternative arrangements were being discussed. Stratagem increased its offer to 163p cash, wishing to ensure that Colonnade was liquidated under the supervision of a different board.

FINANCIAL RESPONSE Colonnade announced the sale of shares in TIP Europe, raising £1.55m. This disposal, it said, brought cash, cash receivables and quoted government securities to £7.1m (or 140p a share). Colonnade used this figure, adding investments and a proposed dividend of 3.2p, to support its claim that Stratagem's 163p value on Colonnade was insufficient.

LEGAL AND/OR POLITICAL On 2 February, Colonnade announced a plan to liquidate and realize 200p per share. It highlighted the accomplishment of its 16.5 per cent investment in Imtec, which owned the successful Laser-Scan company and whose shares had risen sharply. The liquidation plan included a 99p payout in April which required more than 75 per cent shareholders' approval at an EGM called for 5 March. Stratagem announced that it had now built up a holding of slightly more than 25 per cent and intended to block the proposals. An appeal was made to the Stock Exchange to enforce the rule that any stakeholding exceeding 25 per cent must have shareholders' approval. The Stock Exchange responded by insisting that Stratagem receive such approval before using its voting rights. Stratagem criticized the Stock Exchange for stepping beyond its powers, but arranged its own EGM one hour before Colonnade's. Stratagem thereby won its shareholders' approval, and succeeded not only in blocking Colonnade's proposals, but also in defeating the re-election of two Colonnade directors.

Outcome

Stratagem won its bid for Colonnade in March, a few days after blocking Colonnade's own liquidation proposals. At the end of June, Stratagem announced its decision to relaunch Colonnade as a vehicle for investment in Turkey. Argosy Asset Management was to manage the new trust, offering £10m for Colonnade.

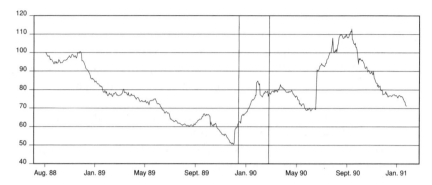

Figure CS32.1 Share performance of Colonnade Development Capital before, during and after takeover bid (relative to FT-A All Share Index)

There is no financial information available for a table in this case study.

CASE STUDY 33: HARTWELL

Target: Hartwell

Motor car and commercial vehicle distribution with ancillary sales and services, heating services and bulk oil distribution, and property investment and development.

Bidder: Oakhill

Wholly owned subsidiary of Saudi Arabian Jameel Group whose interests included car distribution, property, shipping and investment management. It held exclusive rights to distribute Toyota cars in Saudi Arabia.

> **Announcement:** 4 January 1990
> **Value of bid:** £172.4m
> **Defences:** Financial response, legal and/or political
> **Outcome:** BID FAILED

Summary

Hartwell's defence was based on a profit and dividend forecast, property valuation and shareholdings in friendly hands. Hartwell relinquished control after the bid had officially lapsed, saying that the shareholding built up by the predator proved detrimental to the business.

Background

Hartwell was Britain's third-largest motor distributor, with 33 retailing sites. Motor distribution accounted for about 70 per cent of the company's operating profit. In May 1989, Hartwell acquired two motor distributors for £30.2m from the Mercantile Group, which also held a 6.3 per cent stake in Hartwell.

Oakhill was based in Jersey and owned by a Liechtenstein vehicle through an offshore company. Mr Jameel was the sole beneficiary of the Liechtenstein vehicle. Oakhill held meetings with Hartwell directors to discuss possible cooperation and to try to obtain a seat on the board, but all these moves were rejected. The Jameel Group had long-term ambitions to expand in car distribution in Europe and claimed it could bring benefits to Hartwell in terms of depth of management and experience in motor distribution and property. The Jameel Group owned 24.8 per cent of another motor distributor, Trimoco.

Oakhill's all-cash offer comprised 136p for each ordinary share and 124.7p for each convertible preference share, valuing Hartwell at £151.3m. On announcement, Oakhill raised its holding to 19.3 per cent of Hartwell's ordinary shares and 32.1 per cent of its preference shares. The offer was later increased to 155p in cash per ordinary share and 142.1p for every preference share, valuing Hartwell at £172.4m. A full loan note alternative was also introduced. The later offer was on a multiple of 18 times historic earnings. Hartwell claimed the offer was wholly inadequate and said Oakhill was seeking 'to exploit the current weakness in the motor sector to buy Hartwell on the cheap'. Hartwell also pointed out that beneficial ownership of Oakhill could change without disclosure.

Defence

FINANCIAL RESPONSE Hartwell claimed that £1000 invested in the company on 4 January 1980 would have been worth more than £9000 on 3 January 1990, representing a compound annual capital return to shareholders of 24.7 per cent before taking account of dividends. Hartwell predicted pre-tax profits would grow to £12.4m compared with £10.4m in the previous year and the dividend would be lifted by 16 per cent. This estimate was above an earlier BZW (Hartwell's brokers) forecast of £10.5 m. Hartwell's profit forecast included a benefit of £1.2m from reduced pension fund contributions after an actuarial valuation of Hartwell's pension fund turned up a surplus of £16m. Hartwell also revalued its property assets at £124.8m, showing an increase of 28 per cent over book value. Later Hartwell announced it had exchanged contracts for the sale of a site in Oxford for £9.4m which would result in annualized interest savings of about £1.4 m. The value of the property exceeded the earlier asset revaluation.

LEGAL AND/OR POLITICAL Hartwell wrote to the Director General of Fair Trading in an effort to have the bid referred to the Monopolies and Mergers Commission. Its anti-competitive case emphasized Jameel's beneficial ownership of Oakhill through Liechtenstein and the 24.8 per cent held by the Jameel Group in motor dealer Trimoco, but this did not breach guidelines governing competition policy.

Outcome

Oakhill declared the offer for its convertible preference shares unconditional. It held 56.9 per cent of the issued preference shares. At the final close, Oakhill received acceptances representing 43.3 per cent of Hartwell's ordinary shares and accordingly allowed its offer to lapse. However, Oakhill claimed it would eventually gain control of Hartwell on conversion of its preference shares in 1992. According to Hartwell, motor manufacturers had applied pressure to resolve the uncertainty over the company's future which had become increasingly detrimental to the business. Consequently, Hartwell's board decided to accept the offer three months later.

Table CS33.1 Financial performance of Hartwell, 1979–1989

A/c year ending	Div per share	Net eps (adjusted)	p/e ratio*	p/e ratio (sector)†
1979	0.88	4.00	5.4	4.67
1980	1.06	4.63	9.6	5.25
1981	1.06	0.89	10.2	140.68
1982	1.16	2.75	12.8	140.70
1983	1.30	4.05	8.3	140.70
1984	1.48	4.66	8.6	10.16
1985	1.70	5.64	9.9	10.01
1986	1.99	6.14	15.2	11.24
1987	2.25	4.96	15.7	8.58
1988	2.69	8.12	14.3	9.02
1989	3.10	8.62	12.5	10.67

*4 December of year in question.
†Motors.

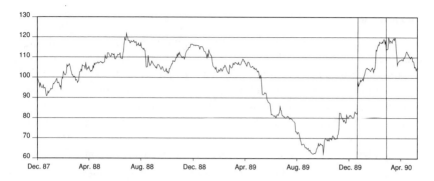

Figure CS33.1 Share performance of Hartwell plc before, during and after takeover bid (relative to FT-A All Share Index)

CASE STUDY 34: NORFOLK CAPITAL GROUP

Target: Norfolk Capital Group

Operator of up-market hotels and clubs.

Bidder: Queens Moat Houses

Operator of middle-range and up-market hotels.

> **Announcement:** 25 January 1990
> **Value of bid:** £184m
> **Defences:** Financial response, corporate restructure
> **Outcome:** BID SUCCEEDED

Summary

Norfolk Capital Group, whose board was divided following an attempted management buy-in by Balmoral International, was subject to a hostile all-share bid from Queens Moat Houses. Norfolk used a property revaluation to show that its assets had been undervalued, but produced defensive disposal plans which lacked credibility. The bid succeeded narrowly, following the resignation of two Norfolk directors and the siding of Balmoral with Queens Moat.

Background

Over an eight-week period, the Norfolk Capital Group had been fighting an attempted management takeover by Balmoral International, a private group investing in hotels and owning 13 per cent of Norfolk. Following Norfolk's poor earnings performance over recent years, Balmoral had provoked a split in Norfolk's board. Two of Norfolk's directors favoured the replacement of their own managing director, Mr Eyles, by the managing director of Balmoral. One of the two, Lady Joseph, was Eyles' former mother-in-law. Her late husband, Sir Max Joseph, had previously run the company. Queens Moat Houses, another hotel operator, announced an all-share bid for Norfolk shortly before a meeting for shareholders to vote on Balmoral's plan. The meeting resulted in the defeat of Balmoral and the election of two new directors who supported Eyles. Despite the split in Norfolk's board, there were no immediate resignations, and there was unanimous rejection of Queens' offer.

Queens offered two new shares for every five Norfolk shares. The offer valued Norfolk at £184m or 44.4p per share, based on the bidder's pre-announcement share price of 111p. On the announcement, Queens shares fell 5p to 106p, and Norfolk shares climbed 4.5p to 40.75p. The offer document promised increased dividends, and described the Queens portfolio which, although very similar to Norfolk's, had been earning far better profits. On 8 February, Queens declared its offer and closing date final, despite the absence of any defence document from Norfolk. At no time in the battle was the offer increased, or supported with a cash alternative.

The defence document was posted on 16 February, the latest permissible date. At the same time, Lady Joseph and her colleague, Tony Good, resigned from the Norfolk board, pledging their combined 8 per cent holding in Norfolk to Queens Moat Houses. In several increments, Queens took its own holding of Norfolk shares to 9.9 per cent, the limit set by the City Panel during any share-for-share bid. On 22 February, Balmoral sided with Queens Moat Houses, bringing the latter's holdings and acceptances up to 31 per cent. When Queens declared that its offer was final and would not be extended beyond 26 February, Norfolk said that an attempt was being made to hurry shareholders. Norfolk suggested that the bidder had no choice but to announce a short timetable because Queens saw its share price falling.

Defence

FINANCIAL RESPONSE Norfolk commissioned a revaluation of its property portfolio, which valued the company's net assets at 53p per share. Thus, it said, Queens was undervaluing Norfolk's assets by 24 per cent. Towards the end of the battle, Norfolk drew attention to the 11 per cent fall in the Queens share price since the offer, and emphasized the widening gap between Norfolk's net asset value and the bid price.

CORPORATE RESTRUCTURE Norfolk estimated that its operating profits for 1989 would advance 45 per cent to £8m, and that its dividend would be lifted 22 per cent to 0.66p (still below the equivalent income offered by Queens). Its pre-tax profits, however, would grow only 4 per cent due to interest costs. It announced the disposal of £75m-worth of assets to reduce its borrowings. These plans were questioned by the outgoing directors, Joseph and Good, in letters they sent to shareholders. There were doubts over planning permission and other legal issues associated with some of Norfolk's property. The timing of the resignations from Norfolk's board weakened the impact of the company's defence document. In the closing stages of the bid, Norfolk announced that unconditional planning permission had been obtained at a site in Edinburgh, and that there was encouraging interest from potential investors in the group's St James' clubs. Norfolk claimed these factors added credibility to its disposals plan, while continuing to increase the company's net asset value.

Outcome

It was suggested that the absence of a cash alternative contributed to the final result being so close. The bid succeeded only on the final day of Queens Moat's tight timetable, when it controlled 52.9 per cent of Norfolk's shares.

Table CS 34.1 Financial performance of Norfolk Capital Group, 1978–1989

A/c year ending	Div per share	Net eps (adjusted)	p/e ratio*	p/e ratio (sector)†
1978	0.31	1.02	13.6	10.73
1979	0.31	0.33	17.4	6.68
1980	0.13	N/A	23.9	7.37
1981	0.05	N/A	50.0	12.55
1982	0.05	0.05	N/A	13.74
1983	0.23	0.43	N/A	15.54
1984	N/A	N/A	431.3	15.80
1985	0.27	0.42	100.3	17.09
1986	0.37	0.82	50.3	17.00
1987	0.45	1.13	54.8	16.57
1988	0.54	0.65	39.8	13.83
1989	N/A	N/A	37.6	15.11

*25 December of year in question.
†Leisure.

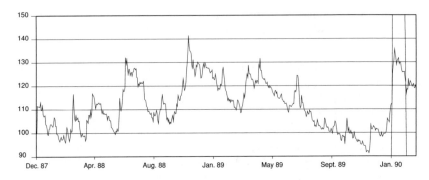

Figure CS34.1 Share performance of Norfolk Capital Group before, during and after takeover bid (relative to FT-A All Share Index)

CASE STUDY 35: CHEMOXY INTERNATIONAL

Target: Chemoxy International

Processor and developer of speciality chemicals.

Bidder: MTM

Processor and developer of speciality chemicals.

> **Announcement:** 2 February 1990
> **Value of bid:** £11.8m
> **Defences:** Financial response, white knight
> **Outcome:** BID FAILED

Summary

MTM made a share-for-share bid for Chemoxy with a cash alternative, and said it would not raise its offer in the absence of any other competitive bid. Both companies were in the chemical processing market, where there was increasing takeover activity. There was always anticipation of a rival bid, and in the following month the Suter industrial holdings company made a higher cash offer which was recommended. MTM allowed its own offer to lapse.

Background

Chemoxy, a manufacturer of speciality chemicals, was the subject of a management buy-out from Carless, Capel and Leonard in 1984. It was floated on the stock exchange for £5.4m in 1987. In spite of its excellent performance in terms of turnover and profits, the company's market capitalization had grown only to about £8m by 1990.

MTM was a chemical processing company which had expanded rapidly over its 10-year life, both organically and by acquisitions. There was a trend towards consolidation by merger and acquisition in the chemical processing sector, as the market was becoming increasingly capital intensive. As well as additional production capacity, MTM was interested in Chemoxy's international business, and its new reprocessing division was particularly attractive in view of growing public concern over economic and environmental issues.

MTM offered 186 new shares for every 100 Chemoxy shares, with a cash alternative of 400p per share. The Chemoxy share price jumped from 268p to 417p in anticipation of a rival bid from any of a number of candidates.

Chemoxy described MTM's bid as unwelcome and inadequate. MTM expressed surprise that its offer had been rejected by the Chemoxy board, and said it would not raise its offer in the absence of any other competitive bid. MTM's offer valued Chemoxy at nearly £12m.

Defence

FINANCIAL RESPONSE Chemoxy's pre-tax profits had increased from £0.6m for 1988 to £1.0m for 1989. It announced a profits forecast for May 1990 of not less than £1.4m. MTM said that such a forecast was not credible in view of Chemoxy's half-year results of £0.5m.

Chemoxy said that this did not take into account special arrangements with the Teesside Development Corporation, which was providing free relocation and a new plant for the company. These arrangements alone were worth anything up to another £8m, and would be jeopardized by a takeover. Chemoxy said that a takeover by MTM might also endanger some of the highly confidential overseas contracts in which it was continually engaged.

WHITE KNIGHT The day after MTM announced a 41 per cent increase in profits, Chemoxy recommended a cash offer from the industrial holdings company, Suter, for £13.45m (450p a share). Suter had for some time announced falls in pre-tax profits due to the decline in property and construction. The company was interested in investing in chemical processing, and had acquired Pentagon Chemicals in May 1989. According to Suter, Chemoxy fitted perfectly with this and other Suter chemical subsidiaries.

The Chemoxy share price rose swiftly to the 450p price. Suter declared a final dividend of 5.6p, lifting its total dividend to 8.4p, an increase of 20 per cent on the previous year's 7p.

Outcome

MTM did not raise its offer, saying that it was not in the interests of its shareholders to overpay for the acquisition of production capacity. Its bid lapsed on 9 March. The Suter offer was declared unconditional a month after it was recommended.

Table CS35.1 Financial performance of Chemoxy International, 1988–1990

A/c year ending	Div per share	Net eps (adjusted)	p/e ratio*	p/e ratio (sector)†
1988	5.75	17.64	13.0	12.41
1989	8.80	27.55	11.8	9.71
1990	N/A	N/A	10.2	9.74

*2 January of year in question.
†Chemicals.

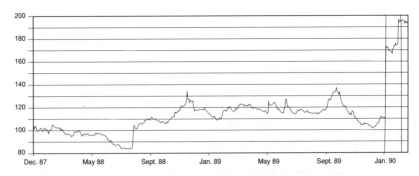

Figure CS35.1 Share performance of Chemoxy International before, during and after takeover bid (relative to FT-A All Share Index)

CASE STUDY 36: LAING PROPERTIES

Target: Laing Properties

Property investment and development.

Bidder: Pall Mall Properties

Subsidiary of Peninsular & Oriental Navigation (P & O), property and shipping, bidding jointly with Chelsfield, a privately owned property company.

>**Announcement:** 5 February 1990
>**Value of bid:** £492m
>**Defences:** Financial response
>**Outcome:** BID SUCCEEDED

Summary

Laing's defence rested on the loyalty of several family trusts, a property revaluation, and criticism of Pall Mall's disposal intentions. The revaluation appeared optimistic in the economic climate, and some selling by trusts enabled the bid to succeed.

Background

Chelsfield was a privately owned property company which had built a 14 per cent stake in Laing and had signalled its interest in making a full bid. The bid was made jointly with P & O through the latter's subsidiary, Pall Mall Properties. P & O and Chelsfield were each putting about £75m into Pall Mall. The balance of funding, about £300m, came from medium-term bank facilities, despite a recent lack of bank support in the property market.

Forty-two per cent of Laing's shares were owned by directors and family trusts, apparently presenting a formidable hurdle to any bidder. However, only about 2 per cent were held directly by members of the Laing family, and there was a conflict of loyalties in cases where directors of Laing were also trustees of the various trusts. Chelsfield increased its stake to over 20 per cent, as the offer of 650p cash per share was announced. Laing shares, which had already benefited from bid speculation, jumped 89p to 653p in response to the events. On 28 March, Pall Mall raised its bid to 725p per share and declared the offer final. This still represented a substantial discount to net asset value. Laing shares rose from 647p to only 660p, reflecting market doubts that the takeover would succeed at this price. Opinions changed, however, following some selling by charitable trusts, fears that Laing shares would collapse if the bid failed, and the accumulation of Pall Mall's own holding to 40 per cent.

Laing accused Pall Mall of exploiting the current depression in the property sector. Laing attached great importance to its overseas diversification: 29 per cent of its portfolio was in Canada and 18 per cent in the US, giving some protection against domestic problems. It dismissed criticism of its asset and dividend growth over the last five years as out of date. Laing criticized the nature of funding for the bid, saying that the £300m of bank facilities would result in a high level of gearing when added to Laing's existing debt of £500m. It inferred that Pall Mall could only have plans to sell the company's assets. Laing asserted that both bidding parties had reputations for buying assets cheaply and selling out at a profit. The acquisition of the Stock Conversion property group by P & O in 1986 was cited as an example. This acquisition had been followed by substantial disposals from the target's property portfolio.

Laing's principal defence, a property revaluation, was not completed in time to be included in its defence document due on 26 February. A week after posting the document, Laing announced a £11m property purchase in Canada, saying that it was not letting the bid distract it from its normal activities. A small dispute arose when Laing announced the discovery of a listening device in its offices during the opening stages of the bid. The effects of the incident were limited, however, following Pall Mall's quick repudiation and Laing's failure to refer the matter to the police at the earliest opportunity. In the closing days of the bid, Laing implied that it was prepared to break itself up rather than let the bidders do it. This suggestion did not help its cause, as it undermined one of its main criticisms of Pall Mall's intentions.

Defence

FINANCIAL RESPONSE The asset revaluation was published on 23 March, together with other financial information. Pre-tax profits were up 18 per cent at £27.8m, and Laing promised a 20 per cent dividend increase for both 1989 and 1990. Its net assets were assessed at 910p per share. This included 67p for surpluses on current developments, a component not usually added in annual valuation calculations, but used recently by Higgs & Hill in its successful defence against Lovell. Laing's valuation was well above market expectations, and slight scepticism in the City moderated the share price increase to 10p. Later, Laing's case was strengthened when it emerged that there were parties interested in purchasing Laing's Canadian property at a 20 per cent premium to asset value.

Outcome

On 11 April, the day before the final closing date, Laing felt forced to recommend the bid in order to avoid what it described as an unsatisfactory deadlock position. Pall Mall had secured about 48 per cent of Laing's equity, including the majority of convertible stock which could be converted into shares the following month.

Table CS36.1 Financial performance of Laing Properties, 1979–1990

A/c year ending	Div per share	Net eps (adjusted)	p/e ratio*	p/e ratio (sector)†
1979	3.28	5.83	23.9	6.73
1980	3.75	7.05	33.6	4.22
1981	4.50	8.75	51.8	5.35
1982	5.00	9.72	27.0	6.61
1983	5.50	12.29	20.8	10.06
1984	6.25	18.57	28.0	9.11
1985	7.00	19.75	27.1	9.74
1986	8.00	23.57	40.5	12.59
1987	9.00	26.53	13.8	17.38
1988	10.25	28.04	14.6	14.19
1989	12.30	29.99	18.5	9.75
1990	N/A	N/A	17.7	8.36

*5 January of year in question.
†Construction and contracting.

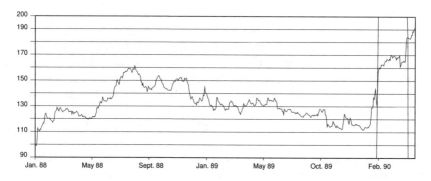

Figure CS36.1 Share performance of Laing Properties before, during and after takeover bid (relative to FT-A All Share Index)

CASE STUDY 37: SKETCHLEY (1)

Target: Sketchley

Dry cleaning, vending and catering, workware and textile services, office services.

Bidder: Godfrey Davis

Textile maintenance, commercial cleaning, laundry services and security services; declining activities in vehicle, contract and portable building hire.

> **Announcement:** 12 February 1990
> **Value of bid:** £138m
> **Defences:** Financial response
> **Outcome:** BID FAILED

Summary

Godfrey Davis made a mixed offer for Sketchley which was rejected as inadequate by Sketchley's board but accepted immediately by at least one major institutional shareholder. Sketchley announced profits far below analysts' already depressing forecasts. Godfrey Davis withdrew its offer.

Background

Godfrey Davis announced a bid for Sketchley, which it said complemented Godfrey's move away from motor-related activities and towards the services sector. Godfrey's gearing would rise to about 200 per cent if the acquisition were to go ahead, but the group announced its intention to dispose of its motor-related businesses to bring gearing down to below the current 90 per cent level.

Godfrey Davis owned no shares in Sketchley. It offered five new shares and 350p for every three Sketchley shares. This valued the company at £138m, or 380p per share. Sketchley shares rose 18p to 382p, indicating the market's initial view that the appearance of a white knight was unlikely. Godfrey Davis shares, however, fell 9p to 149p, and later in the bid to 140p. This reduced the value of Godfrey Davis's offer to 350p per Sketchley share, and implied that a higher all-cash bid might be required from Godfrey Davis or a white knight to accomplish a takeover.

In November 1989, a forecast of £14.8m was given by analysts for Sketchley's pre-tax profits to the year-end in March. This figure was down from the previous year's £17.3m. Godfrey Davis said Sketchley's earnings were distorted by taking £10m reorganization costs below the line and the proceeds of sale and lease-back arrangements above the line.

Mercury Asset Management, a key shareholder with a 17 per cent stake, accepted Godfrey Davis's offer immediately. Other institutions with stakes in Sketchley included M & G and Britannic.

Sketchley rejected the bid as inadequate, saying that insufficient value had been placed on Sketchley's brand name and high-street profile. Its rejection was accompanied by an announcement that its profits to the year-end were likely to be substantially below market expectations. Sketchley's defence document was expected to emphasize its successful withdrawal from America, future benefits from the rationalization and automation of its textile activities, and the growth of its vending business where recent acquisitions were beginning to show gains after a slow start. Sketchley could boast of new workware contracts with British Aerospace and Courtaulds. In addition, added value was being achieved through the new dry-cleaning outlets within Sainsbury superstores, and similar arrangements were being discussed with Asda and Tesco. As the date approached by which its defence document was due, Sketchley obtained the Takeover Panel's permission for a two-day delay.

Defence

FINANCIAL RESPONSE On 1 March when the document was posted, it announced a pre-tax profit forecast of around £6m only, including £2.2m in exceptional profits. Sketchley blamed losses in its vending division and difficulties in its office services business. Earnings per share were forecast to fall sharply from 35.7p to 13.2p, and the yearly dividend from 20.9p to 13p. Sketchley said that although it was disappointed with its forecast, this did not impair the potential for a significant improvement in profits in the future. Sketchley shares fell heavily on the release of the document, before steadying to close a net 6p lower at 349p.

Outcome

After the market had closed on the same day that Sketchley had posted its defence document, Godfrey Davis withdrew its offer. Sketchley shares then fell 98p to 251p. Changes in the company's board seemed likely in order to address mounting shareholder dissatisfaction.

Table CS37.1 Financial performance of Sketchley, 1979–1990

A/c year ending	Div per share	Net eps (adjusted)	p/e ratio*	p/e ratio (sector)†
1979	4.13	N/A	9.5	7.27
1980	6.01	28.59	11.7	7.24
1981	6.76	14.86	20.6	7.11
1982	7.89	20.88	14.4	9.69
1983	9.35	19.22	15.1	12.48
1984	11.20	24.89	15.8	13.80
1985	12.24	17.97	14.7	15.30
1986	14.00	18.74	15.2	15.80
1987	15.20	24.76	14.4	11.18
1988	15.88	22.53	14.1	8.83
1989	17.46	26.68	16.4	9.55
1990	5.43	0.00	14.6	12.44

*12 January of year in question.
†Miscellaneous.

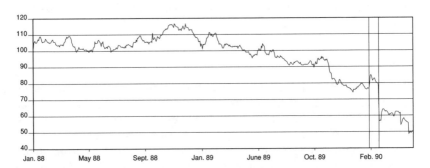

Figure CS37.1 Share performance of Sketchley before, during and after takeover bid (relative to FT-A All Share Index)

CASE STUDY 38: WALTER RUNCIMAN

Target: Walter Runciman

Gas shipping, security, insurance and freight services.

Bidder: Forvaltnings Avena (Sweden)

A quoted Swedish company with activities in property, security and engineering.

Announcement: 23 February 1990
Value of bid: £63.5m
Defences: Financial response, corporate restructure
Outcome: BID SUCCEEDED

Summary

Runciman announced an increase in profits and dividends of about 40 per cent. Its corporate restructuring involved the sale and redevelopment of a site. The bidder secured control by raising the offer in line with Runciman's profits and dividends.

Background

Telfos held a 29.4 per cent stake in Runciman, left over from a hostile bid that lapsed in August 1988. Scottish Amicable Investment Managers with 8.4 per cent had remained loyal during that bid battle. Runciman owned Tann International, the bidder's main competitor in the Scandinavian heavy security equipment market. Runciman and Avena held discussions about merging their security businesses but could not agree over price and voting control. Avena then purchased the 29.4 per cent stake from Telfos and launched a hostile bid. Avena also had a pledge to accept the offer from the National Rivers Authority, which held 4.4 per cent. The offer was made on the basis of 520p per share in cash, which valued Runciman at about £47.8m, a multiple of 17.6 times 1988 earnings.

Avena wanted to become market leader and to exploit economies of scale in heavy security equipment. It criticized the source of Runciman's growth in earnings over the last five years, claiming it had come from reorganization, disposal of underperforming businesses and an upswing in the highly volatile gas-shipping market. Avena pointed to a 49 per cent decline in turnover over the last five years and said the possibility of maintaining growth was limited as the bull run in the shipping market was at an end. Runciman rejected the bid on the grounds that it undervalued the company.

Defence

FINANCIAL RESPONSE Runciman announced preliminary year-end figures above market expectations. Pre-tax profits rose 38 per cent to £5.6m and earnings per share 41 per cent to 41.5p. The dividend was increased by 43 per cent to 15p. Runciman attributed its good results to the shipping division, in which it expected further growth. These figures reduced the offer's multiple to 12.5. Later in the battle Runciman made a profit forecast. Pre-tax profits were expected to increase 34 per cent to £7.5m and earnings per share 33 per cent to 53p. The dividend was forecast to increase 33 per cent to 20p. The company stated that its performance was being buoyed by firm rates in shipping.

CORPORATE RESTRUCTURE Runciman realized some of its property assets by entering into an agreement with Laing Properties. This involved the sale and redevelopment of a site in Hertfordshire occupied by its security division. The joint venture was expected to realize £8.2m by the end of 1992, more than twice its book value. Avena objected to the move and complained that it had not been consulted despite being the largest shareholder in Runciman. Runciman also built up its freight services division by acquiring Cardiff International for £2m with a further consideration of £1.8m payable depending on 1990 and 1991 profits.

Outcome

Avena raised its offer to 625p per share in cash and added a loan note alternative. This offer valued the company at £57.4m and was accepted by Prolific Unit Trust Managers with 5.1 per cent. The next day Avena increased its bid to 690p per share after talking to Scottish Amicable investment managers, who accepted the higher offer. This final offer valued Runciman at £63.5m and Avena now claimed 46.7 per cent. Runciman then recommended the bid and the offer became unconditional immediately.

Table CS38.1 Financial performance of Walter Runciman, 1980–1989

A/c year ending	Div per share	Net eps (adjusted)	p/e ratio*	p/e ratio (sector)†
1980	7.50	23.47	N/A	10.31
1981	11.60	42.26	8.6	8.49
1982	5.00	9.10	4.6	6.38
1983	5.00	5.76	3.6	7.42
1984	5.00	0.90	36.5	18.04
1985	5.00	5.85	64.1	16.38
1986	5.50	17.40	14.1	16.11
1987	6.50	21.32	20.03	20.40
1988	10.50	28.69	10.6	14.41
1989	15.00	41.08	13.5	13.30

*23 January of year in question.
†Shipping and transport.

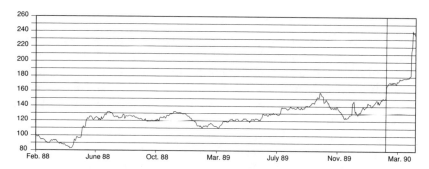

Figure CS38.1 Share performance of Walter Runciman plc before, during and after takeover bid (relative to FT-A All Share Index)

CASE STUDY 39: CAMFORD ENGINEERING

Target: Camford Engineering

Manufacturer of motor components.

Bidder: Markheath Securities

UK investment vehicle (principally property), 49 per cent owned by Adelaide Steamship (Adsteam), an Australian industrial and retailing conglomerate.

> **Announcement:** 1 March 1990
> **Value of bid:** £69m
> **Defences:** Financial response, legal and/or political, poison pill
> **Outcome:** BID SUCCEEDED

Summary

Having built up a holding of nearly 30 per cent in Camford Engineering, Markheath Securities made a hostile cash offer of 305p per share for the company. Camford's financial announcements were spoilt by revelations of its directors' golden parachute contracts. Markheath won control after raising its offer to 330p.

Background

Over a period of two years, Markheath had built a stake in Camford of just under the 30 per cent limit above which a full bid is required. Camford was refusing Markheath a seat on its board. Markheath attacked Camford for having inadequately refocused its business to take account of the growing internationalization of its market-place. It also said that Camford had not managed its property assets and manufacturing capacity as efficiently as possible. As an example, Markheath cited Camford's sale of a site in Stevenage, which it thought could be more quickly and actively pursued. Camford's manufacturing technique itself was not under criticism.

Markheath made a 305p per share cash offer for Camford, valuing the company at £63.8m. Camford's share price rose 64p to 308p, indicating the market's initial expectation that the bid would succeed. By the first close on 23 March, Markheath had gained only 0.35 per cent acceptances. It extended its offer to 6 April, then to 20 April, and finally to 11 May. Only on 24 April, when it considered all defensive financial announcements to have been made, did Markheath raise its offer to 330p.

Defence

FINANCIAL RESPONSE With reference to its Stevenage plant, Camford said that with the planning permission which had been granted, the site's real value was around £26m (against its book value of £4m). This helped boost the company's net assets from £35m to £57m. An independent property valuation of £31m above net book value placed Camford's net assets at £67m, equivalent to about 319p per share. Camford announced a 38 per cent increase in its July interim dividend. This would bring the total dividend up 40 per cent to 8.8p. Later in the battle, Camford promised an additional 15p property dividend which would be paid for at least the next three years. The announcement lifted shares 14p to 321p. Camford separately announced expected pre-tax profits up 37 per cent to £8m, matching almost identical increases over the previous two years. The Camford share price touched 331p.

LEGAL AND/OR POLITICAL Shortly before the first closing date, Camford drew to the attention of the Stock Exchange transactions in Camford shares detailed in Markheath's offer document. The transactions may have been in breach of the Exchange's Class IV rule designed to ensure fair dealing between related entities. Shareholders' specific approval must normally be sought when transactions between two such entities are undertaken. In January 1989, Jomet, another subsidiary of Adsteam, had purchased Camford shares. On 28 March 1989, the same quantity of Camford shares was sold and purchased by Jomet and Markheath respectively, possibly providing Jomet with a profit.

A number of Conservative and Labour MPs lobbied the Office of Fair Trading in protest against possible job losses as a result of foreign takeovers of UK engineering businesses. The Markheath bid did not appear to contravene competition policy, however.

POISON PILL Camford directors had contracts which, if any stakeholding exceeded 30 per cent, allowed them to resign with compensation for their five-year service contracts. Markheath said that this could cost £1.9m in salaries even before bonuses and inflation cover, and represented an unacceptable unknown liability. It argued that the contracts were not in the interests of shareholders, especially since the takeover bid could both fail and leave Markheath with an increased holding. Camford said that the contracts were first agreed in April 1987, before Markheath had any Camford shares. It appeared, however, that Camford had renewed the contracts during the bid, without seeking the approval of shareholders. Markheath announced it was seeking an injunction. Camford waived the contracts, but opinion remained unfavourable. The share price slipped from 320p to 307p.

Outcome

On 9 May, Markheath was able to claim victory.

Table CS39.1 Financial performance of Camford Engineering, 1979–1990

A/c year ending	Div per share	Net eps (adjusted)	p/e ratio*	p/e ratio (sector)†
1979	4.06	12.63	10.0	7.26
1980	1.63	4.33	8.5	5.83
1981	0.00	0.00	9.9	7.20
1982	0.00	0.00	N/A	12.29
1983	0.35	3.29	N/A	10.95
1984	1.05	5.15	15.7	12.44
1985	1.75	8.40	10.9	10.30
1986	2.50	11.58	10.1	11.59
1987	3.00	11.91	12.6	14.06
1988	6.67	13.76	15.2	13.12
1989	8.40	18.48	15.9	12.10
1990	N/A	N/A	11.5	10.28

*1 February of year in question.
†General engineering.

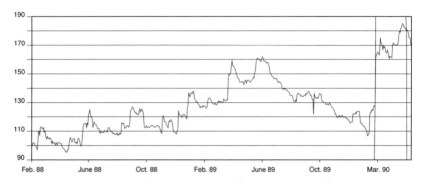

Figure CS39.1 Share performance of Camford Engineering before, during and after takeover bid (relative to FT-A All Share Index)

CASE STUDY 40: SKETCHLEY (2)

Target: Sketchley (2)

Dry cleaning, vending and catering, workware and textile services and office services.

Bidder: Compass Group

Contract catering, health care, building services and security services.

> **Announcement:** 8 March 1990
> **Value of bid:** £106m
> **Defences:** Financial response, poison pill
> **Outcome:** BID FAILED

Summary

Compass made a £106m equity bid for Sketchley. The offer was of substantially less value than the £138m Godfrey Davis bid defeated a week before. Sketchley defeated the Compass bid by appointing outside management team backed by three major institutional shareholders. The new directors were to receive contracts incorporating share option incentives, and compensation if Compass won its bid.

Background

Compass had been approached as a potential white knight during Sketchley's defence against a previous bid from Godfrey Davis. The latter had withdrawn its offer following Sketchley's reduced profits forecast, and Sketchley shares had fallen from 355p to 251p. Compass made a hostile share-for-share bid for Sketchley worth only three-quarters of Godfrey's withdrawn offer. Later the same day, the resignation of Sketchley's chairman was accepted. He had submitted his resignation before the Compass bid.

Compass criticized Sketchley for having too many layers of management, and inadequate financial and operational control of its individual business units. If its takeover were successful, Compass said it would dispose of Sketchley's vending business and seriously review its office cleaning services. Compass offered four new shares for every five Sketchley shares. This valued Sketchley at 292p a share. On the announcement, Compass shares fell 30p to 335p, reducing the value of the offer to 268p. Against the market, Sketchley's price rose 24p to 273p and continued to improve on speculation that Godfrey Davis might return with a new offer.

Sketchley rejected the offer as inadequate and for failing to reflect the real value of Sketchley's market share, brand name, and potential for improved profits. With Compass having been approached as a possible white knight against Godfrey Davis, it seemed that price was the only obstacle to an agreed offer.

Sketchley's shareholders included a number of income funds. Sketchley said that by accepting the Compass offer, shareholders would be giving up the current 7 per cent dividend yield for a 3 per cent yield from Compass. In addition, the offer would leave Sketchley's shareholders with only 30 per cent of the merged group. Compass admitted that many shareholders had kept an investment in Sketchley for its strong dividend yield, but pointed out that Sketchley had been forced to announce a reduction in its 1990 dividend earlier in the month. Compass also showed that its offer gave shareholders a significant capital gain, based on Sketchley's share price before the bid.

Defence

FINANCIAL RESPONSE Sketchley's announcement of only £6m expected profits had earlier caused Godfrey Davis to withdraw its takeover offer. In response to the Compass bid, Sketchley explained that the forecast did not take into account £1.2m of defence costs incurred during the previous battle, or the Chairman's pay-off on his resignation. Accordingly, it said, expected profits were even lower.

POISON PILL Sketchley announced negotiations with three outside management teams. When it was unable to reveal details of any specific proposal in its defence document, it conceded that there might be difficulties in reaching an agreement within the time-scale of the Compass offer. The document, posted on 31 March, argued simply that the group's recovery required a more focused management than Compass could provide. On 6 April, however, Sketchley announced the appointment of a new management team including two executives with renowned expertise. The new directors would be granted share options conditional on Sketchley ceasing to be subject to a bid. In addition, they would each receive £125 000 compensation for 'loss of opportunity' if Compass were successful in its takeover bid. The new team was backed by three institutions with a combined holding of 34 per cent in Sketchley. Shareholders were to vote on the proposal in May, although they would have no say in the compensation package.

Outcome

By 10 April, Compass had received just 1.65 per cent acceptances. The offer was extended to 23 April but, contrary to market speculation, was never increased. The bid lapsed, and Sketchley shares fell to 233p, down 39p on the week.

Table CS40.1 Financial performance of Sketchley, 1979–1990

A/c year ending	Div per share	Net eps (adjusted)	p/e ratio*	p/e ratio (sector)†
1979	4.13	N/A	9.5	6.99
1980	6.01	28.59	13.7	7.88
1981	6.76	14.86	19.9	7.23
1982	7.89	20.88	14.8	10.78
1983	9.35	19.22	16.0	13.67
1984	11.20	24.89	14.6	14.14
1985	12.24	17.97	15.2	15.85
1986	14.00	18.74	16.3	16.10
1987	15.20	24.76	15.4	11.46
1988	15.88	22.53	14.1	8.83
1989	17.46	26.68	18.5	11.86
1990	5.43	0.00	14.0	11.98

*8 February of year in question.
†Miscellaneous.

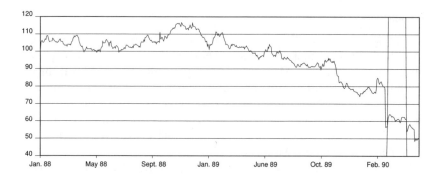

Figure CS40.1 Share performance of Sketchley before, during and after takeover bid (relative to FT-A All Share Index)

CASE STUDY 41: MOLINS

Target: Molins

Manufacturer of machinery for making cigarettes, for packaging and for security printing.

Bidder: Leucadia National Corporation (US)

American company quoted on the New York Stock Exchange with a wide range of interests in financial services and manufacturing.

Announcement: 28 March 1990
Value of bid: £83.0m
Defences: Financial response, legal and/or political, corporate restructure
Outcome: BID FAILED

Summary

Molins claimed the offer was 33 per cent below net asset value and neglected $90m of potential earnings from patents. It appealed to the Takeover Panel about tactics used by the bidder to acquire shares. In preparation for an ensuing proxy battle, Molins appointed new directors and revalued its pension surplus.

Background

Leucadia acquired a 33.2 per cent stake in Molins from IEP Securities for 252p a share. IEP Securities had accumulated the stake in two previous hostile bids for Molins. M & G with 18.8 per cent remained loyal throughout both bid battles. Leucadia bought a further 1.8 per cent of the target and was obliged to extend a mandatory cash offer to acquire the outstanding ordinary shares of Molins at 252p per share. After receiving acceptances of only 0.7 per cent by the second close, Leucadia increased its cash offer to 275p per share, valuing Molins at £83m.

Hambros Bank, Leucadia's adviser, admitted there was little compatibility between the two companies, claiming Molins' main attractiveness was its 'sophisticated engineering capacity' and its potential royalty income from flexible manufacturing systems, first patented by Molins in 1965. These patents were the subject of US legal action. Leucadia criticized Molins' recently announced results. It pointed out that 10p of the 32.4p earnings per share were a result of a holiday from pension contributions, and trading profits had risen by only 2 per cent. It also claimed that profits from Brazilian operations were difficult to recover.

Molins rejected the bid, claiming 'a financially orientated overseas conglomerate with no knowledge of Molins' business or the international markets in which it operates and with nothing to contribute to the development of the group is seeking to acquire Molins on the cheap'. After the bid failed Leucadia attempted to gain control through a proxy vote.

Defences

FINANCIAL RESPONSE Molins claimed the offer was at a discount of 33 per cent to net asset value. Also in its defence document Molins quoted Olliff & Partners, Leucadia's brokers, which recommended Molins shares to investors in January 1990 with a long-term view, believing the shares were worth 485p. Later in the bid battle, Molins predicted a revenue of $90m, before tax, over the next 13 years from patents on its flexible manufacturing systems if litigation in the US was successful. Molins expected a favourable decision by the end of 1991.

LEGAL AND/OR POLITICAL The increased offer by Leucadia was preceded by an announcement from the bidder that it would not raise its bid unless it was able to buy further Molins shares. The announcement enabled Leucadia to buy about 5.4 per cent of the group's equity, taking its holding up to 40.1 per cent. An appeal from Molins to the Takeover Panel, accusing Leucadia of creating 'maximum confusion in the market', failed to gain support.

Defences used before EGM

CORPORATE RESTRUCTURE The managing director resigned and was replaced by another Molins director. Molins also appointed a new director responsible for legal matters and contracts.

FINANCIAL RESPONSE Molins announced interim results for the first six months to 30 June 1990. Pre-tax profits increased by 11 per cent and earnings per share by 27.5 per cent. The interim dividend was raised by 25 per cent. The results included a contribution from a pension fund surplus which was revalued at £85m since its revaluation at £58.4m in the previous year. The net asset value per share was 509p. Turnover fell 23 per cent but trading profits increased by 5 per cent due to an improvement in margins.

Outcome

The bid lapsed with Leucadia holding 45.5 per cent shares and acceptances. Leucadia then bought more shares in the market, increasing its stake to 46.85 per cent, and called an extraordinary meeting of shareholders to vote on a proposal to remove three non-executive directors from Molins and replace them with six Leucadia representatives, giving them overall control. Before the vote, 22 institutions held just over 50 per cent and about 500 individuals, including 200 employees, owned another 1.5 per cent. Leucadia's attempt to install a majority of directors was narrowly defeated.

Table CS41.1 Financial performance of Molins, 1980–1989

A/c year ending	Div per share	Net eps (adjusted)	p/e ratio*	p/e ratio (sector)†
1980	7.90	22.62	5.9	6.17
1981	7.90	14.77	5.8	8.04
1982	7.90	22.65	15.7	11.46
1983	7.90	15.40	12.8	11.26
1984	7.90	7.19	9.8	12.12
1985	7.90	17.12	13.5	10.47
1986	8.70	17.34	18.7	12.97
1987	9.60	21.99	9.6	15.01
1988	9.60	6.92	17.6	13.00
1989	10.50	22.67	9.7	12.58

*28 February of year in question.
†General engineering.

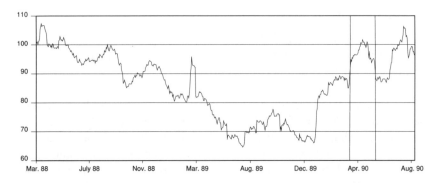

Figure CS41.1.1 Share performance of Molins plc before, during and after takeover bid (relative to FT-A All Share Index)

CASE STUDY 42: CRYSTALATE HOLDINGS

Target: Crystalate Holdings

Manufacturer of electronic components.

Bidder: TT Group

Industrial holdings group. Subsidiaries involved in the manufacture of industrial components, building products, glass containers and other packaging.

> **Announcement:** 30 March 1990
> **Value of bid:** £32.5m
> **Defences:** Financial response, white knight
> **Outcome:** BID SUCCEEDED

Summary

Crystalate relied on a US white knight, Vishay Intertechnology, to fight TT's hostile bid. The two bidders offered similar value for Crystalate shares, but Vishay appeared to offer the better business combination. Vishay's bid was referred to the Monopolies and Mergers Commission, and shareholders chose to accept TT's offer rather than await the uncertain outcome of Vishay's position.

Background

Crystalate had announced 1989 pre-tax profits of £2.9m, down from £3.7m for the previous year. TT began with a 6.6 per cent stake, and offered 7 new shares for every 10 Crystalate shares. At TT's closing price of 123p, this valued target shares at 86p compared with their closing price of 78p. Crystalate's shares were 67p before TT's interest was known. On 17 May, TT introduced a partial cash alternative which valued each Crystalate share at 80.4p.

Crystalate said that TT's offer did not reflect the electronics company's recovery potential. It questioned the prospect of industrial synergy. Before TT introduced a cash element into its bid, Crystalate stressed the uncertainty associated with the all-equity nature of the offer, especially as TT's share price had proved volatile in the past.

Vishay Intertechnology, a US manufacturer of electronic components, announced a rival bid on 25 May. By buying Crystalate, Vishay would eliminate a major competitor and strengthen its European business. Its offer was 80p per share in cash, or equity worth 91p. Crystalate had traded with Vishay for over 20 years. Although Crystalate rejected the bid, it made it clear that it was the terms of Vishay's offer, not the principle of linking with the US company, that was under contention. Crystalate shares fell 4p to 81p.

On 13 July, TT offered a full cash alternative of 85.5p a share. Vishay responded immediately by disclosing its intention to offer 90p in cash, subject to the Crystalate board's recommendation. Crystalate shares rose 10p to 88p. The Vishay offer was indeed recommended a few days later. Vishay's bid was conditional on clearance by regulatory authorities in both the US and the UK. A successful takeover would give the combined group about 50 per cent and 30 per cent of the US and UK resistors markets respectively. Although the bid received clearance with respect to US anti-trust regulations, it was eventually referred to the Monopolies and Mergers Commission in the UK. Vishay promised to offer 93.5p in cash to make up for the delay if the Commission's decision resulted in clearance by November. Vishay said that such an offer would be forthcoming even if the disposal of a small part of its business was required to obtain clearance.

Defence

FINANCIAL RESPONSE On 9 May, Crystalate announced its half-year results. A loss of £0.9m was announced, compared with £2.29m profit the previous year. The loss had been expected, and Crystalate's share price fell only 2p. Blame was placed on falling demand and sharply increased interest payments. Crystalate said that cost reduction and restructuring programmes were under way which, together with a recent disposal completed in March, would allow short-term borrowings to be substantially reduced. The interim dividend was held at 2.2p, a decision described by Crystalate as a gesture of confidence.

WHITE KNIGHT Crystalate did not recommend Vishay's opening bid, which it said did not sufficiently reflect the combined group's strength. Crystalate did recommend Vishay's revised 90p cash bid. When it emerged that Vishay's offer was to be referred to the Monopolies and Mergers Commission, Crystalate urged shareholders to wait for the possibility of considering Vishay's higher cash offer later in the year. Crystalate was not allowed to formally recommend Vishay's intended bid, but reiterated its rejection of TT's offer.

Outcome

TT raised its own Crystalate holding to 37 per cent over a period following its provision of a full cash alternative. With acceptances to 16 August, it could account for over 50 per cent of voting stock. Crystalate accepted defeat a few days later.

Table CS42 Financial performance of Crystalate, 1979–1990

A/c year ending	Div per share	Net eps (adjusted)	p/e ratio*	p/e ratio (sector)†
1979	1.13	2.07	14.5	10.18
1980	1.51	4.16	26.6	10.52
1981	1.75	5.20	18.4	14.77
1982	2.41	8.15	19.3	16.92
1983	3.25	10.51	21.6	17.12
1984	3.85	16.55	25.5	15.08
1985	4.24	16.51	14.4	15.19
1986	5.10	18.37	17.1	15.03
1987	5.85	22.17	16.4	17.61
1988	6.00	13.64	8.7	12.10
1989	6.10	5.84	13.6	14.08
1990	N/A	N/A	11.6	13.48

*28 February of year in question.
†Electronics.

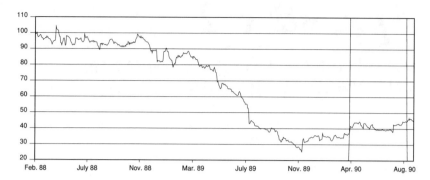

Figure CS42.1 Share performance of Crystalate before, during and after takeover bid (relative to FT-A All Share Index)

Appendix 2

ACTIVITIES OF TARGET COMPANIES ARRANGED BY SIC CODE

Target name	SIC code	SIC code description
A Goldberg & Sons	65600	Mixed retail businesses
Armstrong Equipment	31692	Manufacture of needles, pins and other metal smallwares
	35300	Manufacture of motor vehicle parts
	83960	Holding company
Bassett Foods	61700	Wholesale distribution of food, drink and tobacco
BAT Industries	42900	Tobacco industry
	61700	Wholesale distribution of food, drink and tobacco
	81501	Institutions specializing in investment of securities
	83951	Management consultants
	83960	Holding company
Boase Massimi Pollitt	83800	Advertising
	83951	Management consultants
Business Mortgages Trust	85000	Owning and dealing in real estate
Camford Engineering	32863	Manufacture of machinery
	83960	Holding company
Chamberlain Phipps	45393	Manufacture of miscellaneous dress items
	45570	Household textiles
	48350	Manufacture of plastic packaging
	48360	Manufacture of plastic products
	83960	Holding company
Chemoxy International	25100	Manufacture of basic industrial chemicals
	25670	Manufacture of miscellaneous chemical products for industrial and agricultural use
Coalite Group	14010	Mineral ore refining

Target name	SIC code	SIC code description
	25670	Manufacture of miscellaneous chemical products for industrial and agricultural use
	35210	Manufacture of motor vehicle bodies
	50000	Construction industry
	61100	Wholesale distribution of agricultural and textile raw materials and live animals
	61200	Wholesale distribution of fuels, ores, metals and industrial materials
	61300	Wholesale distribution of timber and building materials
	63000	Commission agents and commodity brokers
	74000	General sea transport
	77003	Storage and warehousing
Colonnade Development Capital	81500	Other financial institutions (general)
Consolidated Gold Fields	21000	Extraction and preparation of metalliferous ores
Crystalate Holdings	34542	Manufacture of electronic equipment (other)
	83960	Holding company
De La Rue	47544	Other printing
	83960	Holding company
Dixons	61500	Wholesale distribution of household goods and hardware
	61900	Wholesale distribution (other)
	85000	Owning and dealing in real estate
DRG	32893	Mechanical engineering (other)
	46720	Manufacture of shop and office fittings
	47280	Manufacture of other paper and board products
	48350	Manufacture of plastic packaging
Gateway Corporation	61000	Import and export dealers
	83960	Holding company
Habit Precision Engineering	24600	Manufacture of abrasive products
	32221	Manufacture of hard-tipped and other cutting tools
	83960	Holding company
Hartwell	50000	Construction industry
	61200	Wholesale distribution of fuels, ores, metals and industrial materials
	61480	Wholesale distribution of motor vehicles, parts and accessories
	83960	Holding company
	85000	Owning and dealing in real estate
Hestair	35102	Manufacture of commercial vehicles
	47231	Manufacture of notepaper
	48320	Plastics semi-manufactures
	49410	Manufacturer of toys and games
	83954	Miscellaneous business services
	83960	Holding company
	85000	Owning and dealing in real estate
	95100	Hospitals, nursing homes
Higgs & Hill	50000	Construction industry

Target name	SIC code	SIC code description
Ketson	61480	Wholesale distribution of motor vehicles, parts and accessories
	65100	Retail distribution of motor vehicles and parts
	83960	Holding company
Laing Properties	85000	Owning and dealing in real estate
Lambert Howarth Group	45100	Footwear
	61000	Import and export dealers
	83960	Holding company
Local London Group	83400	House and estate agents
	83962	Central offices of enterprise with mixed activities
	85000	Owning and dealing in real estate
Marina Development Group	36102	Building or repairing pleasure boats and yachts
	76300	Supporting services to sea transport
Meat Trade Suppliers	41263	Processing of animal by-products
Metal Closures Group	22452	Rolled, drawn, extruded and other semi-manufactured aluminium products
	31643	Manufacture of metallic closures
	48350	Manufacture of plastic packaging
	48360	Manufacture of plastic products
	83960	Holding company
Molins	32443	Manufacture of tobacco-processing machinery
	32760	Manufacture of printing and bookbinding machinery
	32863	Manufacture of machinery
Norfolk Capital Group	66200	Public houses and bars
	66500	Hotel trade (general)
	83950	Business services
	83960	Holding company
	85000	Owning and dealing in real estate
Norton Opax	47544	Other printing
Pearl Assurance Group	81502	Institutions specializing in granting of credit
	82000	Insurance (general)
	83954	Miscellaneous business services
	83960	Holding company
	85000	Owning and dealing in real estate
Piccadilly Radio	97411	Radio and television services
Red Funnel	74003	Sea transport by domestic and coastal routes
Ricardo Group	37100	Manufacture of measuring and precision instruments
	83702	Technical services
	94000	Research and development
Sketchley	43702	Other textile finishing processes
	45340	Manufacture of work clothing and mens' and boys' jeans
	61600	Wholesale distribution of textiles, clothing, footwear and leather goods
	66401	Catering contractors
	67200	Repair of footwear and leather goods
	92300	Cleaning services
	98110	Laundries
	98120	Dry cleaning and allied services

Target name	SIC code	SIC code description
Tilbury Group	50000	Construction industry
United Scientific Holdings	22452	Rolled, drawn, extruded and other semi-manufactured aluminium products
	31643	Manufacture of metallic closures
	48350	Manufacture of plastic packaging
	48360	Manufacture of plastic products
	83960	Holding company
Walter Runciman	34330	Manufacture of alarms and signalling equipment
	61900	Wholesale distribution (other)
	74001	Sea transport by deep sea routes
	77002	Freight broker and freight transport
	82000	Insurance (general)
Ward White Group	45100	Footwear
	61600	Wholesale distribution of textiles, clothing, footwear and leather goods
	64600	Retail distribution of footwear and leather goods
	64800	Retail distribution of household goods and hardware
	65100	Retail distribution of motor vehicles and parts
	65600	Mixed retail businesses
	83960	Holding company

INDEX